Gay-affirming theology

An explicit exposé

Bruce Benson

Heart Wish Books

Gay-affirming theology

An explicit exposé

Copyright © 2022 Bruce Benson

All rights reserved

This includes the right to reproduce any
portion of this book in any form

Published by Heart Wish Books
Cambridge, Massachusetts

heartwishbooks@gmail.com

All Bible quotations are the author's paraphrase unless marked

Scripture quotations marked KJV are from
the King James Version in the public domain

Library of Congress Control Number: 2022903475

ISBN: 978-0-9998039-3-6

Nonfiction – Religion – Biblical Studies – Exegesis & Hermeneutics
Nonfiction – Religion – Christian Life - Relationships

Other books by Bruce Benson

AHA moments from the Bible

Jehovah's Witnesses Hate Jehovah

The Bible on Abortion: The shedding of innocent blood

The Catholic Church: femme fatale

Bible Talk: 50 literal drawings explained

Try my Bible Quiz

Speaking in tongues: Shamana bo-ho roe-toe

Joseph Reflects Jesus: Lifegivers

Otros libros del autor en español

Teología de la validación gay: Una exposición explícita

Momentos AJÁ de la Biblia

Los Testigos de Jehová odian a Jehová

La Biblia sobre el Aborto: El derramamiento de sangre inocente

La Iglesia Católica: mujer fatal

Charla sobre la Biblia: 50 dibujos literales explicados

¡Prueba mi cuestionario bíblico!

Hablar en lenguas: Shamana bo-jo ro-to

José refleja a Jesús: Dadores de vida

Contents

Glossary ... 9

Chapter one
What might the devil have said to Eve? ... 11

Chapter two
Can the common person understand? ... 17

Chapter three
How would I describe gay-affirming theology? ... 25

Chapter four
Why did I use indelicate language? ... 29

Chapter five
Who are the Apiscopal priests? ... 33

Chapter six
Did Jesus say anything about homosexuality? ... 41

Chapter seven
Is Jesus a bad tree? ... 45

Chapter eight
Who's responsible for gay people's suicides? ... 49

Chapter nine
Who is our Guide?... 57

Chapter ten
Are gay people born that way? ... 61

Chapter eleven
Why couldn't you pray away the gay? ... 65

Chapter twelve
Who is Peter of the Gāəthēs? ... 73

Chapter thirteen
If straights can divorce – then why can't gays be gay? ... 85

Chapter fourteen
Were David and Jonathan gay? ... 89

Chapter fifteen
Should you partake in a gay pride parade? ... 101

Chapter sixteen
Where's Paul of the Gāəthēs? ... 105

Chapter seventeen
Why can't you be Gay Christian? ... 113

Chapter eighteen
Were Ruth and Naomi gay? ... 117

Chapter nineteen
Are two men as good as a man and a woman? ... 125

Chapter twenty
Should a man look like a woman? ... 129

Chapter twenty-one
Did Jesus heal a man's male lover? ... 137

Chapter twenty-two
What's Sodom? ... 145

Chapter twenty-three
Where's Jesus of the Gāəthēs? ... 153

Chapter twenty-four
Is Jesus inclusive? ... 167

Chapter twenty-five
What's a J•Lite? ... 175

Glossary

Arg — argument

Believer — a Christian, someone who belongs to Jesus Christ

Bəthē — Bible-affirming theologian

Gāəthē — gay-affirming theologian

Gay — a slang word for homosexual

Gay okay — okay with homsx

Gay people — people who say gay is who they are – who see nothing wrong with being gay, and no reason to change

Gentiles — generally, anyone who does not worship the one true God

GRV — the Gāəthē Revised Version of the Bible

Hetsx — noun, heterosexuality

Hetsx — adjective, heterosexual

Hetsxl — noun, heterosexual

Holy — God is holy, holy, holy. He is 100% pure, good, just, and fair

Homsx — noun, homosexuality

Homsx — adjective, homosexual

Homsxl — noun, homosexual

Interp — interpretation

Jesus of the Gāəthēs — a Jesus created by the gāəthēs who says whatever the gāəthēs tell him to say

KJV — the King James Version of the Bible

NT — New Testament

OT — Old Testament

Paul of the Gāəthēs — an apostle named Paul, who was created by the gāəthēs to say what the gāəthēs want him to say

Peter of the Gāəthēs — an apostle named Peter, who...well, you know

Pharisees — a religious sect that hated Jesus

Redeem — a redemption center redeems a soda bottle when they pay a nickel to buy it back. Jesus redeems repentant sinners. Jesus had to pay with His blood, His life, to buy us back

Relate — relationship

Repentance — a real change brought about by grief over offending God

Sac — sacrifice

Saved — if you trust in the death of Jesus on the cross as the payment for your sins, if He is your Lord and Savior, and you truly believe that Jesus rose from the dead, then you are saved from death in hell

Sin — we sin when we disobey God's laws   1 John 3:4

Smsx — same-sex

Sodomites — residents of Sodom

Straight — a slang word for heterosexual

Trans — people who don't identify with their birth gender

The Word of God — the Bible, from Genesis to Revelation   John 1:1-18

Chapter one

What might the devil have said to Eve?

The devil – Another lovely day in the Garden.

Eve – Yes, my good sir.

The devil – God is great.

Eve – He sure is.

The devil – Praise Him.

Eve – Amen, brother.

The devil – Oh, before I forget, could you help me?

Eve – Yes, of course.

The devil – There's a nasty rumor going around.

Eve – What is it?

The devil – I'm sure it's just a big misunderstanding. And forgive me for asking, but –

Eve – Go ahead. You can ask me anything.

The devil – That's a good girl. So, what I'm hearing is that God won't let you eat from every tree in the Garden. Please, tell me it's not true.

Eve – No, God said we can eat from every tree in the Garden. But there's one tree that God said we're not allowed to eat from.

The devil – You must not have heard Him correctly.

Eve – Why do you say that?

The devil – I'm the local tree-affirming theologian.

Eve – I knew there was something special about you.

The devil – How could you tell?

Eve – I saw your colorful stole, and that halo over your head.

The devil – Be assured now. I have your best interest in mind.

Eve – God said we'll die if we eat from that tree.

The devil – I promise you, my dear – you truly, truly, will not die.

Eve – But it's right there in Genesis 2:17.

The devil – Oh, the clobber passage.

Eve – Clobber?

The devil – You use the Bible to clobber tree-eaters because you're ashamed of your own desire to eat from the tree. You hate tree-eaters because they have what you want.

Eve – I don't hate them. I love them.

The devil – Now think, Eve. When you say it's wrong to eat from that tree, you make tree-eaters feel bad. Stop being a bully. Put away your Bible and you'll be free to love.

Eve – That sounds right. But still, I know what I read.

The devil – Your simple reading of the Bible is worthless. You can't possibly know what the writer of Genesis meant. Most scholars agree that ancient minds had different ideas about the tree than we do now.

Eve – God said it, and –

The devil – Stop! Away with this – God said it and I believe it business. Biblical literalist! Instead of engaging in a conversation, you just want to tell the rest of us what the Bible says. You're guilty of the sin of arrogance – thinking you know how God feels.

Eve – Sorry. I can see now that I have unrealistic ideas about the Bible. It's wrong to think we can know for sure what the Bible says.

The devil – I knew you'd come around.

Eve – I just don't want to disobey God.

The devil – Now you're being legalistic. The Bible isn't a rule book. And it's not like you're murdering somebody.

Eve – I think I'll play it safe. There's plenty of other trees in the Garden. I don't need to eat from that one tree.

The devil – Psychologists have found that avoiding one tree can cause unhealthy feelings like guilt and shame that lead to self-harm.

Eve – I don't know.

The devil – Are you going to deprive yourself of the benefits of the tree because of one verse?

Eve – Wait. Did you say benefits?

The devil – Some new information has surfaced.

Eve – But God only spoke negatively about the tree.

The devil – Yes, He did. But we've discovered the good way to eat from the tree. It proves that when God said don't eat, He meant don't eat in the bad way.

Eve – Tell me about the benefits.

The devil – Yes, my lady. There's a secret about the Garden.

Eve – What's the secret? Tell me now. Please!

The devil – There's a way of enjoying the Garden that God didn't tell you about. When you eat from the tree, your eyes will open and you'll know the secret.

Eve – How will the tree make that happen?

The devil – There are amazing properties in the tree that will turn a common person like you into a god.

Eve – A god?

The devil – Yes, dear. Look at that tree. See how beautiful it is. Go ahead. God won't kill you. God is good. It is written – God is love.

Eve – Oh yes, you're right. It's the most beautiful tree I've ever seen. The fruit looks delicious. And I wouldn't want to deprive myself of the benefits you speak of.

The devil – Just relax now. This won't hurt a bit. It will be very nice, very dignified. You'll make the rules. You'll be God. Eat, my love.

Chapter two

Can the common person understand?

> You can't understand what God said about the tree unless I explain it to you.
>
> The Devil

> You can't understand what God said about homsx* unless I explain it to you.
>
> Reverend Burpcider

---

* See the glossary on pages 9 and 10

A very important Reverend said the common person can't understand the five or six verses in the Bible that deal with homsx.*

There's an odd thing though about Reverend Burpcider – I believe that was his name. If the common person says gay okay, then the Reverend says the common person can understand.

How many verses do you need?
Do you know how many verses God used when He told Adam and Eve He'd kill them if they ate from the tree? One. One verse!

- Here's what God said to those two common people –

> I'll kill you if you eat from that tree.
> God, Genesis 2:17

What could God possibly have meant by that?

God expected Adam and Eve to understand what He said, and obey it. They ate from the tree and God killed them just like He said He would.

- Here's what God said about homsx –

> I'll kill you if you do homsx.
> God, Leviticus 20:13

God expects you to understand that and obey it. If you do homsx, then He will kill you, just like He said He would. God is a Man of His Word.

God used three verses to say He'd kill rapists. That's three less than the six verses Burpcider said weren't enough for the common person to understand homsx. Maybe Reverend Burpcider would like to ask God how in the world He thinks three verses is enough for a common rapist to understand it's wrong to rape a woman.   Deuteronomy 22:25-27

Does Mr. Burpcider think bestiality's okay because God only used a few verses to condemn people who have sex with animals?
                                                Leviticus 18:23; 20:15-16

Is the Reverend right? Do only really smart people like him get to understand the Bible? No. The person with the highest I.Q. in the world can't understand the Bible. Then who can?

Only those who want to obey Jesus –

> I will reveal Myself to
> those of you who never let go of
> My commandments – and obey them,
> because you're the ones who love Me.
> Jesus, John 14:21

Jesus is the Bible. If you have a sincere desire to obey Jesus, then He will let you see Him in ways that those who refuse to obey Him will never experience.

Jesus will remove the covering from your eyes. Then you'll be able to see His commandments clearly (the commandments of Jesus are the same as God's commandments).   Matthew 5:17-48; John 1:1

Jesus has a strong emotional attachment to those of us who obey Him. It's an affectionate love, a fondness. He welcomes us into a warm friendship –

> If you do whatever I tell you to do
> then you are My friends, the ones I love.
> Jesus, John 15:14

Burpcider doesn't love Jesus –

> If you refuse to do what I say,
> it means you don't love Me.
> Jesus, John 14:24

> If you don't love the Lord Jesus Christ
> – you're marked for death.
> 1 Corinthians 16:22

There's two kinds of people – the natural and the spiritual
When I was sixteen I got invited to have dinner with some young Christians who lived communally. When I mentioned to them that I wanted to be a vegetarian they became very upset. I asked them what was wrong and they showed me 1 Corinthians 2:14 in the KJV, which says – the natural man receiveth not the things of the Spirit of God.

The word man in that verse is the Greek word anthropos. It means people – both male and female. It's where we get the English word anthropology. And the word natural doesn't mean a vegetarian or someone who lives in a forest. It's the Greek word psuchikos, pronounced soo–kee–kos. Jude used it too.

In Jude 1:19, the word sensual is psuchikos. Jude said the sensual, or natural person, is someone who pretends to be a Christian. They reject the things of the Spirit of God because they want to stay under the control of their lower nature – the animal appetites. Their only goal in life is to fulfill their godless cravings. Instead of natural and spiritual, we can say the two kinds of people are animal and spiritual.
Jude 1:10, 17-19

Why can't Burpcider learn?

> If you live your life under the control of
> the animal appetites, then you can't learn,
> because these things are understood spiritually.
> 1 Corinthians 2:14

If the most educated people in the world don't have understanding from God's Holy Spirit, then they're no better than unthinking animals.

> You who are devoid of God-given spiritual
> discernment might be held in high esteem by
> the world. But when you die, God sees your
> death as no different than the death of
> the pigs that people slaughter for food.
> Psalm 49:20

Jesus only gives His Holy Spirit to those who obey Him –

> If you love Me and do as I say,
> then My Father will love you.
> And We will come to you
> and make you Our permanent home.
> Jesus, John 14:23

The reason Burpcider says you can't understand is because he can't understand. If Reverend Burpcider had his eyes opened by Jesus and his heart renovated by God's Holy Spirit, then he'd show the evidence of a genuine conversion. He'd stop billing himself as an openly gay pastor, and He would apologize to all the people he misled.

Burpcider's saying the common person will get the Bible wrong if they study it on their own. That's been the prime directive of cults ever since the devil told Eve she'd get it wrong. Burpcider is stealing the Word of God from people – he's stealing Jesus. That's the devil's job.

> There are people along the path
> who start to hear the Word of God.
> But immediately, the devil comes along
> and takes away the Word
> that was planted in their hearts.
> Jesus, Mark 4:15

When did Eve start to doubt what God said about the tree? It was when someone came along and told her why God said don't eat. Who was that? It was Reverend Devil. But that old devil lied to her.

God never told Adam and Eve why He said don't eat. And He never invited them to ask why. What lesson can we learn from Eve's mistake? Don't listen to Reverends.

Reverend Burpcider puts doubt in your mind by telling you why God said don't do homsx. But that old devil is lying to you.

Burpcider's problem is self-pride

Reverend Burpcider says – well, you know, only a few of us elites can interpret the real meaning in the Bible. Burpcider can't stand the idea that God would give understanding to a common person. He says to God – how could you give those nobodies understanding? I have all the degrees, positions, titles, and honors. I want to be the one to tell them what's what. I want them to kiss my feet.

> A stupid person has a better chance
> than someone who thinks they're smart.
> Proverbs 26:12

Reverend Burpcider hates you. But you're in good company. The first followers of Jesus had their Burpciders too. The so-called religious authorities knew the apostles weren't Divinity School graduates. So it was shocking to them when they saw the fearlessness with which the apostles Peter and John publicly proclaimed the truth about Jesus.

Acts 4:13; See John 7:15

Burpcider's saying salvation is out of reach because the Creator's writing skills are lacking. If the common person can't understand – do homsx and die, then they can't understand – believe in Jesus and live. Then God would be unjust for sending people to hell. But God is not unjust. God is righteous, loving, and impartial.

Deuteronomy 32:4; John 3:16;
Acts 10:34-35; 2 Peter 3:9

Anyone can understand – if they want to. If you were on an island by yourself and you found a Bible, you could read it and understand it. Why? Because God can use His wireless transmitter to send the understanding directly into your mind. The apostle John wrote this to every Christian, to every true believer –

> You've received the Gift from Jesus.
> The Gift that Jesus gave you lives in you.
> So you know everything you need to know.
> And you don't need any Burpciders to teach you.
> 1 John 2:20,27

Reverend Burpcider thinks he knows better than Jesus –

> I thank You, oh Father, Lord of Heaven and Earth,
> that You teach the truth to childlike people,
> and You hide it from those who
> think they're educated and clever.
> Yes Father, in Your wisdom You know it's right
> for You to give out Your blessings that way.
> > Jesus, Luke 10:21

Oh, the irony.

The point Jesus is making is that education and cleverness, without God's blessings, amounts to what you find in your cat's litter box. You don't need a big brain. You need a soft heart and godly reverence.

> Circumcise therefore the foreskin of your
> heart, and be no more stiffnecked.
> > God, Deuteronomy 10:16 KJV

> God shares His secrets
> with those who reverence Him.
> > Psalm 25:14

God will find everyone guilty who does not obey the five or six verses in the Bible that deal with homsx. He told us about homsx in a way that's impossible to misunderstand.

An unusual thing happened in one episode of the TV show Columbo. The lieutenant made an arrest. But Columbo was a common person. When he started to tell the suspect his rights, he fumbled for the words. He didn't know the Miranda warning. But Columbo knew what really mattered – he figured out who the murderer was. He had a gift for that.

A lot of people that the world calls common become Christians. Christians are the common people of the world. But we have a gift for figuring out what really matters – what God said in the Bible.
> 1 Corinthians 1:17-31; 2:1-16; 1 John 2:20,27

Chapter three

How would I describe gay-affirming theology?

Insane
What if people said you should eat through your anus and poop out of your mouth – and they made a mouth-pooping theology out of it?

Offensive
Gay-affirming theologians are pulling down their pants, bending over, spreading their cheeks, and showing their butthole to God.

Untruthful
Suppose someone told you they're an oceanologist who spent fifty years exploring the world's oceans – and they can assure you that there are no fish there. Would you say they have a different interpretation? No. You'd say they're lying to you.

Chapter four

Why did I use indelicate language?

You have no part
with the deadly deeds
of the devil and his people.
God is holding you responsible to
do the work of putting them to shame.
Pull the covers off them so everyone
can see what they're really doing.
                    Ephesians 5:11

The apostle Paul told Christians not to use indelicate language.

Ephesians 5:4

But Paul used the word dung to describe the spiritual credentials he had before he became a Christian. Philippians 3:8 KJV

Did he break his own rule? No. It's a matter of intent. Paul said don't use indelicate language – but give thanks instead. He was talking about everyday conversation. I've written an exposé. My indelicate language has a purpose. I hate using it in everyday conversation. I love giving thanks instead.

God said –

> The names of those whom the other
> nations worship must never be heard
> coming from your mouth.
> God, Exodus 23:13

But God Himself said the names Baal, Dagon, Molech, Chemosh, Ashteroth, and Diana. Numbers 22:41; Judges 16:23; 1 Kings 11:5,7; Acts 19:24

The prophet Elijah said this to the children of Israel –

> How long will you hop back and forth?
> Make up your mind.
> If God is God, then follow Him.
> But if Baal, then follow him.
> Elijah, 1 Kings 18:21

And Elijah ridiculed Baal worshipers
They'd just spent hours calling out – oh Baal, hear us. But Baal didn't answer. So Elijah told them maybe Baal couldn't hear them because he was busy with other things. But Elijah didn't break God's command to not let the name Baal be heard coming from his mouth. Elijah did it to expose Baal for the nothing that he is. 1 Kings 18:27

And I didn't break God's command to not use indelicate language. Why? Because I used it to ridicule gay-affirming theology and expose it for the obscene blasphemy that it is.

God used indelicate language in the Old Testament –

God told the spiritually unfaithful children of Israel that they were like a young woman who lets men molest her by squeezing her breasts.
Ezekiel 23:21

God told Israel they were like a prostitute who spreads her legs for every man that comes along.   Ezekiel 16:25

God said they lusted after lovers who have penises like donkeys and emissions of semen like horses.   Ezekiel 23:20

Most books about gay-affirming theology take it seriously, as though it's a legitimate field of study. I won't contribute to the deception with another sanitized version. You need to know how evil it is. The right response is one that's gross, graphic, and over the top.

You'd hate it no matter how I wrote it.

Chapter five

Who are the Apiscopal priests?

> The Apiscopal Church
>
> invites you
>
> to stay in your sin.
>
> The Very Wrong Reverend
>
> Tiffany Windows
>
> wolf in sheep's clothing

Apiscopal priests are the new smiling face of tree-affirming theology. Or as they call it, gay-affirming theology.

There's a fatal flaw in gay-affirming theology. God is not gay-affirming.

The Ironic priesthood.

The greatest hypocrite of all-time is the devil. Hypocrites are actors in costumes pretending to be what they're not – and pretending to not be what they are. The devil deceives by wearing pious clothing. That's why he slithered into Eden disguised as a beneficent theologian.

Apiscopal priests disguise themselves in sanctified clown costumes. They look like a comedy troupe doing a parody of Christians.

Jesus had to deal with liturgic psychopaths. They were in religious cliques called the scribes and Pharisees. And they had things in common with the Apiscopal priests. 2 Corinthians 11:13-15

Jesus said the scribes and Pharisees love it when they're out in public and people call out to them – Teacher! Teacher! • The Apiscopal priests give themselves official titles for people to call them by. Matthew 23:7

Jesus said to the Pharisees – you make bigger boxes to keep your Bible verses in, and bigger ribbons to put on your robes. You do everything for one reason – so people will gaze at you in awe. • Apiscopal priests drape themselves in worthless rags – full-length gowns, larger hats, longer scarves, and better tinsel. Jesus said beware of the scribes who love to walk around in long robes. Matthew 23:5; Mark 12:38

Jesus said – you scribes and Pharisees, you look innocent – but on the inside you're full of hypocrisy and illegality. You're like bleached tombs. They appear beautiful on the outside – but on the inside, they're full of dead bones and every filthy thing. • What are the Apiscopal priests hiding behind their facades? Matthew 23:27-28

Pharisees and Apiscopal priests get you to sin the same way the devil got Eve to sin – by attacking the Word of God. They dethrone the Word of God as the supreme ruling authority. 2 Timothy 3:13

Jesus said the Pharisees took away the saving power in God's Word by adding their own words. The devil and the Apiscopal priests add their own words when they say you won't die if you eat from their tree.
Matthew 15:9; 23:13; Mark 7:13

> Every tree that was not planted
> by My Heavenly Father
> will be ripped out by its roots.
> Jesus, Matthew 15:13

The Apiscopal priests serve up death with a smile, just like their father, the devil, did to Eve. Jesus defeated death when He died on a cross and then rose from death three days later. And Jesus defeated the devil.

The devil has been sentenced to death for his crimes. When Jesus returns He will carry out the execution. Here's a verse by verse account of what happened and what will happen –

> Lucifer, you shiny one – how did you fall out of Heaven?
> You were like the light that appears in the morning.
> Isaiah 14:12

> You were in Eden, the Garden of God.
> and you were clothed with every precious stone.
> Ezekiel 28:13

> The serpent was craftier than any beast of the field
> that the Lord God had made.
> Genesis 3:1

> Satan knows how to make himself
> look like an angel of light.
> 2 Corinthians 11:14

Through one man – Adam, sin and death
infected all of us, because all of us
disobeyed when Adam disobeyed.
> Romans 5:12

God repays disobedience with death.
> Romans 6:23

Death came through a man.
Resurrection from death also came through a man.
In Adam all die. In Christ all can be made alive.
> 1 Corinthians 15:21-22

Jesus took on a body made of flesh and blood
because His children take on bodies of flesh and blood.
Jesus took on that human body like ours so He could die.
And by dying, Jesus took away the devil's ability
to lead God's children to death through sin.
Jesus freed those who were held captive
for their whole lives because of their fear of death.
> Hebrews 2:14-15

The Lord God said to the serpent
– because you did this,
hatred will exist between you and Eve,
and between your children and her Child.
You will strike her Child,
but He will shake it off like a slight bruise.
Then He will crush your head.
> Genesis 3:15

After you've been taken down from your
lofty dreams, you'll descend into the prison
– to the furthest part of the deepest hole.
> Isaiah 14:15

> I'll bring fire out from your insides. It will engulf you.
> I'll turn you to ashes in the dirt. And I'll make sure that
> everyone who knows you sees what I do to you.
>> God, Ezekiel 28:18

> And I, John, saw an angel coming down from Heaven.
> He had the key to the bottomless pit in his hand,
> and a big chain. And he captured the dragon,
> that old serpent, who is the devil and Satan,
> and bound him for a thousand years.
>> Revelation 20:1-2

> Then the devil who deceived them
> was thrown into the lake of fire and sulfur.
>> Revelation 20:10

Eve didn't know she was talking to the world's greatest liar.

The Seducer vs. The Inexperienced One

Welcome sports fans to the Grapple in the Garden. This one looks like a real mismatch. I don't see it going past the first round. It should be an easy victory for the Seducer as he goes against a first-time fighter.

> I think about how the devil cheated Eve out of her virtue.
> And I lay in bed at night, sleepless,
> worrying that the same thing could happen to you
> – that you might let false teachers twist your minds,
> and lead you away from a single-hearted devotion to Christ.
>> The apostle Paul, 2 Corinthians 11:3

> There are people who claim to be speaking for Me.
> But I never sent them. I don't even know them.
> And I'm proud of you, My children, because you
> investigated them, and you found out that they are liars.
>> Jesus, Revelation 2:2

> The devil and his children are liars.
>> Jesus, John 8:44

The Apiscopal Church
welcomes everyone
to come in
and be led astray.
Reverend Randy Quack
goat herder
Reverend Robin Salvation
liar

Chapter six

Did Jesus say anything about homosexuality?

Gāəthēs think this way –

- Jesus never said the word homsx
- Therefore, Jesus is gay okay

He didn't say the word incest either.

Jesus said porneia – in Matthew 15:19 and Mark 7:21. In those two verses, the KJV calls porneia – fornications. Jesus said porneia defiles a person. Jesus is not porneia okay.

What's porneia?
Porneia is any sinful sex. It's # 4202 in the Strong's Concordance. How do we know what's sinful? First John 3:4 gives us the definition of sin. We sin when we break God's law.

God's law condemns homosexuality. That means Jesus is not gay okay.

Jesus never said don't burn your kids as sacrifices to the god Molech. He didn't need to. He'd already said it in the Old Testament.

Jesus condemned incest in the Old Testament – in Leviticus, and in the New too – in First Corinthians, chapter five. Why did Jesus condemn it in First Corinthians but not when He walked the earth? Because there was a man in the church in Corinth who was doing incest. When Jesus walked the earth He was asked by the Pharisees if they could do wife swapping. They didn't ask Him if they could do incest.
                                        Leviticus 18:6-16; 20:11-12; Matthew 19:3

Wasn't that God who condemned homsx, incest, and child sac in the OT, and Paul who condemned incest in the NT? Yes, it was. But Jesus is the Word of God. Jesus is the OT and the NT. The words of Leviticus and First Corinthians are just as much the words of Jesus as the words He spoke when He walked the earth.   John 1:1,14

It was Jesus who condemned homsx in the books of Leviticus, Matthew, Mark, Romans, and First Corinthians.

Chapter seven

Is Jesus a bad tree?

Jesus Christ came to the world to save sinners.
1 Timothy 1:15

Here's how gāəthēs add one plus one to get gay okay –

- The Bible says homsx is sin
- That makes gay people feel bad
- Therefore, the Bible says gay okay

More gāəthē math –

- Jesus said bad trees produce bad fruit
- Gay people feel bad when Bəthēs say homsx is sin
- Therefore, Jesus said Bəthēs are bad trees

Gāəthēs had to maul Matthew 7:15-20 to make it agree with their conclusion. That's where Jesus said – bad teachers are like bad trees that produce bad fruit – and good teachers are like good trees that produce good fruit.

Gāəthēs say Jesus is warning that one of the worst sins a person can commit is to make gay people feel bad by saying homsx is sin.

Then gāəthēs use that interp to conclude that anyone who says homsx is sin is guilty of doing violence to gay people. Laws are being enacted to silence Bəthēs by making it a crime to say homsx is sin.

In verse 19, Jesus said every tree that does not produce good fruit will be thrown into the fire. When Jesus says fire, He means hell.

Gāəthēs say Jesus is warning that if anyone refuses to produce good fruit by saying gay okay, then He will send them to hell. Next, they accuse anyone who won't say gay okay of doing violence.

It's not violence when Christians won't affirm what you do. Our speech, conscience, and religion are commanded and given by God.

Jesus did not say adultery okay
A mob wanted to stone a woman to death because she committed adultery. Jesus rescued her from them. If the gāəthēs are right about their bad tree interp, then Jesus must have said to the woman – go, and commit adultery some more. But Jesus didn't do that. He said to the woman – go, and sin no more. John 8:11

The gāəthēs might say – did you see what Jesus did? He said adultery is sin. That woman might feel guilt, shame, and despair. Oh, the bad fruit. How could Jesus be so cruel? She just barely escaped with her life from an angry mob who wanted to kill her for being an adulteress. What was Jesus thinking by calling adultery a sin? Jesus is a bad tree.

On another occasion, Jesus said – repent, or die in hell. Today, people would be demanding that Jesus apologize. They'd call it violence and hate. Jesus never apologized for saying that. Jesus never said – oh, did that hurt your feelings? Sorry, I take it back – stay in your sins and go to hell. Luke 13:3,5

When Jesus said – repent or die in hell, He was trying to make you feel bad. And if Jesus was here today, He would make you feel bad by refusing to address you by your choice of pronoun.

Jesus said His Holy Spirit will call everyone sinners. Will the gāəthēs ask for a law to silence God's Holy Spirit? John 16:8

The Bible never says it's a bad thing to feel bad about your sin. The only way you can be saved is if you feel bad about your sin. Gāəthēs make a fatal mistake. They blame Bəthēs for making them feel bad. They should blame themselves for not feeling bad.

> If you feel bad like the unrepentant sinners of the world feel bad, then you're just working out your eternal death.
> But if you feel bad because you sinned against God,
> then you've worked out your salvation – you'll live forever.
> 2 Corinthians 7:10

Chapter eight

Who's responsible for gay people's suicides?

Gāəthēs know their theology is obviously fake, having no basis in reality. So, they need to cloud your judgment. That's why they start their books with a sad story –

> A teenage boy was sexually attracted to other boys.
> But his Christian parents told him the Bible says homsx is sin.
> That caused the boy to have feelings of guilt, shame, and despair.
> As a result, he started using drugs, and died of an overdose.

Gāəthēs cash in on gay people's suicides. They use them to toy with your emotions – to trick you into accepting their misbegotten theology. They divert your attention away from the real causes of the teen's death by rousing your anger against his Christian parents.

Tell me, gāəthēs – if a thief took drugs and died, would you blame his Christian parents because they showed him the eighth commandment?
Exodus 20:15

> Keep your mind fixed on the laws that I've given you this day.
> And etch them into the minds of your children.
> God, Deuteronomy 6:6-7

Don't blame the parents because they told their son that homsx is a sin. They obeyed God. Parents will be held accountable by God if they don't discipline their children and teach them right from wrong.

> God's vengeance will come down from Heaven
> upon all those who hide the truth.
> Romans 1:18

What if a teenage girl was having sex with boys, and her Christian parents told her the Bible says it's a sin? If she took drugs and died would you blame the parents because they didn't affirm her behavior?

> A parent who refuses to correct their child is the
> enemy of their child. But when a parent loves
> their child, they warn the child right away.
> Proverbs 13:24

The other reason gāəthēs start their books with a sad story is because they want to control Christians. They say – a gay youth committed suicide because of your teachings – so stop saying homsx is a sin or you'll cause more deaths.

If Christians stopped saying homsx is sin, would gay people stop committing suicide? No. Why not? Because Christians aren't responsible for gay people's suicides. Who is? They are.

There's a flagrant omission in the gāəthē's sad stories. They never talk about the teenager's responsibility. He chose homsx and drugs, and it cost him his life.

Gāəthēs don't teach teens to confess their sins. Instead, gāəthēs teach them to blame their parents. They're really teaching them to blame God, just like the devil taught Eve to do. Gāəthēs tell teens they're heroic if they disobey God, dishonor their parents, and feel no remorse for their rebelliousness.   Genesis 3:5

You can't blame your Christian parents

> You have no excuse.
> God, Romans 1:20

When king David sinned, God sent the prophet Nathan to David. Nathan told him a story that made him come to his senses and face the reality that what he did was wrong. And how did David respond?

David didn't turn to drugs, and he didn't blame Nathan. He put the blame where it belonged – on himself. David said – I've sinned against God – have mercy on me, oh God, and wash me thoroughly from my iniquity – cleanse me from my sin because I acknowledge my sin.
                                                   2 Samuel 12:1-13; Psalm 51:1-3

The teenager in the Gāəthē's sad story was blessed with Christian parents. He was given that gift but did nothing with it. Jesus told a story about people that He gave gifts to. Some appreciated the gifts and diligently used them to do good work for Him.

And Jesus said to them – well done, My good and faithful servants.

Matthew 25:14-23

There was another person in the story. Jesus gave them a gift. But they did nothing with it. And when Judgment Day came, what did that person do? They blamed Jesus. But Jesus said they were lazy and evil.

Matthew 25:24-25

Jesus said – take from them the gift that I gave them. Give it to the people who appreciated what I gave them and made use of it. And take this worthless person and throw them into the darkness outside My kingdom, where there is weeping and gnashing of teeth.

Matthew 25:26-30

Only sinners get saved
The message of Christianity is that God saves sinners. That's the first thing you need to know. The job of Christians is to tell people about sin so they can repent of their sin and be saved. Christianity exists because of sin. That's why there's a Bible. That's why there's Jesus. That's why churches have crosses. Sin! Our sin is why Jesus was crucified.

Gay people can't get saved if they think they don't need saving. The ones who get saved are those who hear the truth from the Bible and feel guilt, shame, and despair – because they realize they've sinned against God. That's why Christians have to say homsx is sin.

The lesson Gāəthēs leave out of their sad stories is the seriousness of sin and the fatal consequences of sin. Gāəthēs are gay people's worst enemies. Bad trees tell you lies to make you feel good. Gāəthēs want gay people to feel good now and feel bad later.

Christians want you to feel bad now, and feel good later – forever.

Christians tell hetsxls the same thing we tell homsxls – God holds them accountable for their sexual sins. Do you gāəthēs blame Christians because hetsxls take their lives? No, of course not. You just don't want us to say homsx is a sin.

Tell me Gāəthēs, are you driving hetsxls to suicide by telling them the Bible says adultery is sin? Or are you calling evil good by affirming their adultery? 1 Corinthians 6:9-10

What if Christians were gay-affirming?
If every Christian in the world said gay okay, it woudn't change a thing. Hearing the truth from the Bible is not what drives gay people to suicide. Being gay is what drives gay people to suicide.

Gay people feel shameful, despairing, and suicidal because they've gone as far away from God as a person can go. They know deep down that they're engaging in the ultimate rebellion against God. They left God for homsx. Then God let go of them. Romans 1:25-28

Truth from the Bible gives life
Banning the Bible would ban the cure. Less Bible means more sexual immoralty, more drugs, more crime, more mental illness, more suicide. The only thing that changes a person's heart is Bible teaching. It's the only hope for gay people and straight people.

Thank God if you live a country where the Bible is still freely available and taught.

If you want to talk about the Bible and Jesus, then you have to acknowledge the reality that Jesus said there's a place called hell. And the Bible says God will send gay people to hell. Anyone who tells you otherwise is lying to you. They're not speaking for God. And despite what they might say, they don't love you. Matthew 5:30; 10:28; 23:33; 1 Corinthians 6:9

The ones who love you are those who warn you. Christians are gay people's best friends because we tell you the truth.

If you break God's law and do homsx – bad things will happen to you. Deuteronomy 28:22,58-61

When Jesus said repent or die, He meant it. He said it twice. Don't test that. You'll be sorry if you do. Luke 13:3,5

You don't have to commit suicide because you've done homsx. You can repent. God will show you His amazing love and mercy and welcome you with open arms. We can be forgiven for any sin if we go to Jesus.

Jesus is the only hope for gays and straights. The real Jesus that is, not the fake ones.

Do you feel bad because Christians say homsx is sin? You should feel bad that Jesus had to be crucified because of your homsx.

If you're gay and suicidal, you need to humble yourself and repent.

> God's commandments are a lamp.
> His law is light.
> And warnings are the way
> to eternal life.
> > Proverbs 6:23

> If you dismiss warnings,
> it means you hate yourself.
> A smart person responds
> to warnings by obeying.
> > Proverbs 15:32

Chapter nine

Who is our Guide?

In *Jehovah's Witnesses hate Jehovah*, our Guide was the truth found in the Bible that Jesus is God. In *The Bible on Abortion*, our Guide was the truth found in the Bible that a fetus is a person.

Now I'll introduce you to our Guide for this book –

- There's no lawful homsx in the Bible

Gāəthēs created a character called Gay Christian. They sneak him in at the beginning of their books. So, they start with a false premise. Therefore, every conclusion in their books is false.

No one in the Bible has ever seen Gay Christian.

He wasn't there when God created marriage. God only created hetsx marriage. Gay Christian wasn't on Noah's ark. God told Noah to take just eight people on the ark – four hetsx couples. There were no gay people on Noah's ark. And all the animals on the ark were hetsx.
Genesis 1:27-28; 2:18-25; 7:1-16

When I was eleven, I was a fan of Napoleon Solo, one of the main characters in the TV show, The Man From U.N.C.L.E.

The boy across the street told me he had photographs of Robert Vaughn, the actor who played Napoleon Solo. I couldn't wait to see them. But when he showed me the photos I could see that he'd cut out pictures of Robert Vaughn's face from a magazine and pasted them over the faces of people in his family's photo album.

Gāəthēs claim they can show you photos of Gay Christian in the Bible. I'll show you how to look closely at those photos so you can see what the gāəthēs did. They drew pictures of Gay Christian's face and pasted them over the faces of people in the Bible.

Chapter ten

Are gay people born that way?

Yes. Gay people are born that way. We're all born that way. We all have sinful desires because we're all descendants of Adam.   Romans 5:12

Here's Gāəthē and Bəthē to discuss Acts 8:26-40 –

Gāəthē – God told Philip to baptize a gay man into the Church.

Bəthē – Why do you say the man was gay?

Gāəthē – The Bible says he was a eunuch. Kings used them to guard their women. So, eunuchs had to be special kind of men – men who had no interest in women – men who were born that way – gay men.

Bəthē – No. Eunuchs were castrated men. Their testicles were removed. That's why they didn't have sex with the king's women. Castrated men could be trusted. So, they were placed in high positions.

The word eunuch is # 5631 in the Strong's Concordance.

In Genesis 39:1 we read of a man named Potiphar who worked as an officer for the Pharaoh of Egypt. The word officer in that verse is the same Hebrew word as eunuch. It's # 5631 in the Strong's Concordance. The same number as the word eunuch.

But Genesis 39:7 says Potiphar had a wife.

The word eunuch was also used for a trusted man in a high position who was not castrated. So, there's no reason to think the eunuch Philip met was castrated or gay.

Gāəthē – We can see from ancient literature that eunuchs were gay men. There's even a sex manual that defines the word eunuch as a man who pursues other men for sex.

Bəthē – You're going outside the Bible for your theology.

Gāəthē – Okay, let's go to the Bible. In Matthew 19:12, Jesus said homosexuality is not a sin because gay people are born that way.

Bəthē – Jesus didn't say that. The conversation had nothing to do with homosexuality. The Pharisees asked Jesus if a man could divorce his wife for any reason. Jesus said no. And His disciples said – if that's how it is, then it's better to be single. Jesus responded to that comment.

Jesus said singleness is only given to three kinds of men. He called them eunuchs. He said there are men who were born eunuchs, and men who are made eunuchs by others, and men who make themselves eunuchs to devote themselves to God.

The born eunuchs are men who don't have sex because of something they were born with. Jesus didn't say what it is. He did not say they were unable to have sex because they were gay. Jesus never said a eunuch is a gay man. The Bible never says a eunuch is a gay man.

Why would gāəthēs want Gay Christian to be a eunuch? Jesus defined eunuchs as men who do not have sex. If Jesus meant those who are born eunuchs are born gay, then He would be saying it's given to a man who's born gay to remain unmarried, which would mean no same-sex marriage.

If there was such a thing as a man who was born gay, he would be acting in obedience to God's law by staying unmarried. But Jesus wasn't talking about a gay man. God does not make men gay.

In Matthew 5:17, Jesus said He did not do away with the law. If He said something now that was completely contrary to the law – that God makes men gay – then His disciples would have asked Him to explain.

But we read nothing of that. After Jesus told them about the three kinds of eunuchs, the conversation ended.

Jesus never affirmed homosexuality before or after this conversation. He's not going to affirm it now by making some veiled reference to men being born gay. Jesus would never sin against God or cause anyone to sin by affirming homosexuality or any other sin.

Chapter eleven

Why couldn't you pray away the gay?

I'm strong enough to do all things
because of the power Christ gives me.
   Philippians 4:13

Sometimes at my street ministry, men say to me –

I asked God to take away the gay, but He didn't – so I'm gay.

That's like saying –

I asked God to take away my desire to look at women with lust, but He didn't – so I look at women with lust.

> Woe to those who blame their Maker.
> Isaiah 45:9

Oh, boo, hoo. Poor baby. God didn't take away your gay.

Well, guess what, He didn't take away my gay neither, or my desire to look at women with lust, or my desire to get back at people who hurt me, or to gossip, or covet, or be depressed, etc., etc., etc.

When you became a Christian, the gay person you used to be died on the cross with Christ. Then you rose up from death with Christ and became a new person. But a Christian's old sins still live in the body made of flesh.

Paul wrote about these things in Romans 6:1-23 and 7:14-25.

So, if you are truly saved, then what you're experiencing now is the old gay desires in your flesh. God doesn't take those from a Christian until our flesh body dies. That's when He gives us eternal spiritual bodies that have no sin, and never will.　　　　　1 Corinthians 15:42-58

Until then, it's our job, with God's help, to wage war against the sins in our flesh – to take up the armor of God – and fight like a child of God until our last breath.　　　　　　　　　　　　　　Ephesians 6:10-18

> If you live for your flesh, then you will die.
> But if you're slaying the flesh through the Spirit,
> then you'll live forever.
> Romans 8:13

Here's the problem – you quit.

> If they were one of us,
> then they would have stayed with us.
> But they walked away. And when they did that,
> they showed that they're not really one of us.
> 1 John 2:19

So, you have to examine yourself. Are you really saved? Did you take up the sword of the Spirit – the Word of God? You did read the Bible? Then what? Jesus said we prove we're really His disciples if we keep on staying in His Word. God rewards those who search for Him.

> John 8:31; 2 Corinthians 13:5; Ephesians 6:17; Hebrews 11:6

Do you think you study the Bible because you go to your church's services and Bible studies? That's not studying the Bible. You need to set up a place at home. You need a desk or table, lamps with bright bulbs, pens, paper, and a comfortable chair.

Get two six-foot-tall bookshelves and put them on either side of your chair, facing you. Now fill them up with books to use in your study. The first ones you need are a KJV Bible and a Strong's Concordance. Then add more books – ones that show you the words of the Bible in the original languages – and study-Bibles – and books about figures of speech in the Bible – and commentaries.

Now you need three things –

- God's blessings
- unending hard work
- a face set like flint

You should always be looking forward to getting back to that desk. That should be the place where you get peace, comfort, and joy – and more and more knowledge and wisdom from God. If you truly believe, then as you go on, you'll feel God's presence, and you'll notice that God is cleansing you and changing you. Start with 1 Corinthians 6:11.

You've got to be creative, use your imagination. Come up with exciting ways to dig into the Bible. When I first started studying the Bible, I created questions that taught a lesson.

That led me to a street ministry where I quizzed people. And they would ask me questions – hard ones. That made me dig into the Bible to find the answers. Then I turned the answers to those questions into pamphlets and displayed them at the street ministry for people to take. Now I write books about the Bible.

I go for walks to stimulate my mind, and I write down my thoughts. There's paper, pens, and a flashlight in my bed in case I wake up in the middle of the night with ideas. And I wait a couple of minutes before I get up in the morning, to see what God has put on my mind.

You have to discipline yourself. Don't ever start your day without first spending some time studying the Bible, and praying, and thanking God. And ask God. Ask Him – what do You want me do today? Doing those things first can make all the difference in how you deal with what comes at you during your day.

Can you say this to God? –

> I've treasured up Your Word in my heart
> because I don't want to sin against You.
> Psalm 119:11

Fighting your gay urges is hard work – a tremendous, all-out effort. It will take time, sacrifice, and determination – for a lifetime. Jesus said if you want to follow Him then you need to decide if you can pay the price – everything you have.   Luke 14:25-35; 1 Corinthians 9:24-27

Instead of saying what God didn't do, ask yourself what you didn't do. Becoming a Christian is not like getting a library card.   Hebrews 12:1

> We must go through much anguish
> to enter into the Kingdom of God.
> Acts 14:22

Did you fight? And did you keep fighting?

> Maintain a vigorous struggle
> in the Christian faith.
> > 1 Timothy 6:12

> Suffer through difficulties with me,
> as a good soldier of Jesus Christ.
> > The apostle Paul, to Timothy
> > 2 Timothy 2:3

You're a Christian, and sometimes you have intense homsx desires. You feel like you're going mad, like you're possessed.

> Wait for the Lord.
> Have courage.
> He will strengthen your heart.
> Wait, I say, for the Lord.
> > Psalm 27:14

> In this world you will go through
> pain and suffering.
> But be courageous,
> because I have conquered this world.
> > Jesus, John 16:33

Jesus told Christians to do this –

> You must pray constantly,
> and not be cowards.
> > Jesus, Luke 18:1

> The cowardly will have their
> place in the lake that burns
> with fire and brimstone.
> That's the second death,
> the death of the soul.
> > Revelation 21:8

> If you faint when distress comes,
> your strength is small.
>> Proverbs 24:10

Can't pray away your gay? Immanuel can!

Jesus prayed to the Father –

> Scrub them clean with Your truth.
> Your Word is truth.
>> Jesus, John 17:17

Do your part –

If you want God to take away your gay, then you have to agonize to enter through the narrow gate.   Matthew 7:13-14

> Keep praying and don't quit
>> Jesus, Luke 18:1

> If you're truly saved, then you'll show it by enduring until the end.
>> Jesus, Matthew 24:13

> Be faithful until death.
>> Jesus, Revelation 2:10

Chapter twelve

Who is Peter of the Gāəthēs?

Excerpts from the GRV –

> God said to Peter of the Gāəthēs – if I say
> something's holy – then stop calling it unholy.
> Acts 10:15 GRV
> Gāəthē Revised Version of the Bible

Then Peter of the Gāəthēs said –

> When God gave the Holy Spirit to gentiles,
> He taught us that gentiles are no different than us.
> So, we must not call the gentiles unholy.
> And we learned something else from that experience.
> We must not call gay people unholy either.
> And we must not burden gay people by asking them
> to obey Old Testament laws. We couldn't obey
> those laws and neither can anyone else.
> Peter of the Gāəthēs, Acts 15:7-10 GRV
> Gāəthē Revised Version of the Bible

Here's Bəthē to ask the question –

Bəthē – Who is Peter of the Gāəthēs?

PetG – I'm the chief apostle of Jesus of the Gāəthēs. And call me PetG.

Bəthē – So, PetG. You've made an incredible claim about gay people.

PetG – Yes. Gays are the new gentles.

Bəthē – Gentles?

PetG – What? Oh, sorry. Gentiles.

Bəthē – What led you to that conclusion?

PetG – Experience.

Bəthē – Tell me about it.

PetG – It started with a voice.   Acts 10:13

Bəthē – A voice?

PetG – Yes, God's voice.

Bəthē – And what did God say?

PetG – He told me to let the gentiles become Christians.
                                                                        Romans 2:10-11; 3:29

Bəthē – You weren't letting them become Christians?

PetG – No.

Bəthē – Why not?

PetG – We didn't like them.   Acts 10:28; 22:21-23

Bəthē – Did God say anything else?

PetG – He told me to go to a gentile's house.

Bəthē – What happened there?

PetG – The gentiles received the Holy Spirit.

Bəthē – You must have been surprised.

PetG – Astonished.

Bəthē – So, the gentiles were in?

PetG – There was a problem.

Bəthē – What?

PetG – People love their factions.

Bəthē – Who?

PetG – The schismatics – a band of self-righteous sectarians.
Acts 11:1-3; Galatians 2:12

Bəthē – What was their problem?

PetG – They said the gentiles had to do two things before they could become Christians.

Bəthē – What things?

PetG – Circumcise their penises and obey the Old Testament law.

Bəthē – Why did they want them to do that?

PetG – Because they're cold-hearted legalists.

Bəthē – Legalists.

PetG – That's right.

Bəthē – What did you do?

PetG – We had a meeting. There was myself and others on one side, and the schismatics on the other.
Acts 15:1-29

Bəthē – What did you say to the schismatics?

PetG – I told them about the voice, how God sent me to some gentiles and they received the Holy Spirit.

Bəthē – Did they listen?

PetG – No.

Bəthē – How did the meeting end?

PetG – A man named James had an idea.

Bəthē – What was it?

PetG – He said – let's choose four Old Testament laws for the gentiles to follow.

Bəthē – What were the four?

PetG – James said we'll tell the gentiles to –

> abstain from pollutions of idols, and from fornication, and from things strangled, and from blood.
> Acts 15:20 KJV

Bəthē – Did it work?

PetG – Yes, everyone agreed.

Bəthē – But PetG, what does that have to do with gay people?

PetG – Well, we were bigoted against gentiles. But then I had the experience of seeing them receive the Holy Spirit. So I thought – if we were wrong about gentiles, what if we're wrong about gay people too? So I went out and talked to gay people.

Bəthē – What did they say?

PetG – They said they have the Holy Spirit.

Bəthē – And?

PetG – I thought, if God gives the Holy Spirit to gay people, then who are we to say they can't be Christians? God showed me that I needed to rethink the old established traditions of prejudice against gay people.

Bəthē – What did you do?

PetG – I welcomed them into the Christian Church.

Bəthē – You did?

PetG – Of course.

Bəthē – Why?

PetG – I can't have a double standard.

Bəthē – Why not?

PetG – Gays are no different than gentiles.

Bəthē – Why don't you respect the authority of the Bible?

PetG – I do.

Bəthē – The Bible clearly forbids homosexuality.

PetG – That's what I thought. But because of my experience I was able to reconsider that interpretation and see that it was wrong. I didn't need a Bible verse to tell me what happened. I went by what I saw, gay people telling me they had the Holy Spirit.

Bəthē – But the law clearly says – no homosexuality.

PetG – We don't want to be legalists like the schismatics – forcing gay people to obey Old Testament laws. We can't burden gay people with the old law. We couldn't obey it and neither can anyone else.

Bəthē – If you have God's Holy Spirit, then it's not a burden to obey God's law. It's a joy. Psalm 119:162; 1 John 5:3

PetG – No one's ever told me that before.

Bəthē – There's some problems with your argument.

PetG – Give me a specific.

Bəthē – God told us in both the Old and New Testament that gentiles would join the Christian church. God never said that about gay people. In fact, the Bible says unrepentant sexually immoral people are not to become members of the Christian Church.
       Isaiah 49:6; Acts 9:4,15; 26:17-20; 1 Corinthians 5:1-13

PetG – Gentiles sin too.

Bəthē – But it's not a sin to be a gentile. It is a sin to be gay.

PetG – Gentiles didn't even know the Old Testament laws. They must have been breaking lots of them. But God gave them the Holy Spirit.

Bəthē – When someone joins the Christian church, whether they be gentile or not, or gay or straight, they're expected to repent – change their mind about their sin, and acknowledge and confess their sin. Gay people refuse to do that. That's the problem with saying you're gay.

PetG – But what about my experience?

Bəthē – You came to the wrong conclusion from your experience. Your conclusion contradicts the clear teachings of the Bible.

PetG – How?

Bəthē – The schismatics were legalists, but not for the reason you think.

PetG – No?

Bəthē – Obeying God's laws isn't legalism.

PetG – Then what's legalism?

Bəthē – They wanted the gentile's penises circumcised, right?

PetG – What's the harm in that?

Bəthē – The harm is in the reason why.

PetG – What reason?

Bəthē – To bring the gentiles back to the covenant of Moses.

PetG – How do you know that?

Bəthē – The apostle Paul wrote the epistle to the Galatians to fight against the legalism of the schismatics. Paul said if you try to earn your salvation by obeying the law, then your circumcision becomes a sign that you've returned to the covenant of Moses.

Paul said if you do that, it means you've never trusted in the death of Jesus on the cross as the payment for your sins – you were never saved.
Galatians 5:2-4

PetG – But you said obeying the law is not legalism.

Bəthē – What matters is why you obey.

PetG – What legalism did the schismatics teach?

Bəthē – The legalism they taught was – obey the law to be saved. That's the burden no one can bear. It's a false gospel.

PetG – Gospel?

Bəthē – The Gospel is what Jesus did to make a way for us to be saved.
1 Corinthians 15:1-4

PetG – What happens to people who teach a false gospel?

Bəthē – They're anathema. Galatians 1:8-9

PetG – What's that?

Bəthē – It means they're headed for destruction.

PetG – What's the right reason to obey the law?

Bəthē – Because God said to. And out of gratitude.

PetG – Gratitude for what?

Bəthē – For what Jesus did.   2 Corinthians 9:15

PetG – What did He do?

Bəthē – God let people spit in His face and crucify Him.
Psalm 22:16; Matthew 26:67; 27:35

PetG – Why?

Bəthē – Because we disobeyed the law.
Isaiah 53:10; Hebrews 9:26; 1 John 3:4

PetG – So, I got it wrong.

Bəthē – Yes. And when you say the old law is done away with, you're being deliberately vague to lead people astray. Law was not done away.

PetG – Then what was?

Bəthē – The covenant of Moses.

PetG – You mean there's a new covenant?

Bəthē – Yes. Read Hebrews 6:20 to 10:39.

PetG – Homsx wasn't in James' four laws.

Bəthē – James told the gentiles to obey four Old Testament laws –

- don't sacrifice to idols – Leviticus 17:7

- don't eat blood – Leviticus 17:10-12
- don't eat strangled animals – Leviticus 17:13-14
- don't commit fornication – Leviticus 18:1-24

PetG – Okay.

Bəthē – I want to look at the fourth one.

PetG – Fornication. It means prostitution.

Bəthē – It means a lot more than that.

PetG – Does it?

Bəthē – The Greek word James used is porneia.

PetG – What does it mean?

Bəthē – It means every kind of sexual sin listed in the Old Testament. That means James was not doing away with the old law, as you call it. And it means homosexuality is still a grave sin.

PetG – But gay Christians have the Holy Spirit.

Bəthē – No. You can't be gay and Christian.   Matthew 7:13-23

PetG – James said the gentiles just had to obey those four laws for a little while. That's why Christians can be gay and eat pork.

Bəthē – Leviticus eleven says don't eat pork.

PetG – That's because they didn't have refrigerators when Leviticus was written. And besides, the pigs we have now are clean.

Bəthē – There are no clean pigs.

Bəthē – Would the gentiles be free to murder, steal, and rape? No, of course not. No one is free to disobey God. You're wrong. James did not do away with God's law. Christians love God's law.   Psalms 119

PetG – Okay, Mr. Bəthē, tell me something, why <u>did</u> James say the gentiles had to obey those four laws?

Bəthē – Well, it wasn't so they could become saved by obeying them, as the schismatics said they must.   Acts 15:1,5,24

Trying to become saved by obeying the law is what Peter was talking about when he referred to the yoke that no one can bear, Acts 15:10. James agreed with Barnabas and the apostles Peter and Paul, that salvation is a gift from God, by God's grace, and you can only receive salvation from God in one way, and that is by your genuine faith, and not by getting your penis circumcised, or by doing any other act, including obeying God's law.   Acts 15:7-9,11-12

The schismatics hated the idea that the gentiles could join their club, become Christians, so easily, just by believing in the Lord Jesus Christ. They wanted the gentiles to become like them first, with circumcised penises, and obeying the law of Moses – in order to <u>become</u> saved.

And the schismatics had convinced many of the people in the Church to think like them, to see the gentiles as unworthy to be Christians. That was mostly because of their sinful prejudice, Acts 10:28; 11:1-3. But it was true that the gentiles had been freely engaging in sexual immorality, and other practices that were disgusting.
     Ephesians 4:17-20

So, James gave the gentile Christians those four laws. Obeying those laws would make the gentiles pleasing in the sight of the Christians who saw the gentile's former lives as disgusting. And in that way, the Church, which was in its infancy, would be held together, and not split in two. It pleases God when His people are one.
     Psalms 133:1;
     Galatians 3:26; Ephesians 4:1-6; Hebrews 13:1

Chapter thirteen

If straights can divorce – then why can't gays be gay?

Gāəthēs are like children. All the other kids are getting divorced – why can't we be gay?

Why? Because divorce and homsx are two different things.

- God permits divorce and remarriage in some cases.

See Ezra 10:1-12 and Deuteronomy 7:3-4.

Study Exodus 21:10-11; Deuteronomy 21:10-14; 24:1-2; Jeremiah 3:8; Matthew 19:9; and 1 Corinthians 7:15

(No, you can't divorce your wife because she eats like a cattle drover.)

- God never permits homsx.

Don't let gāəthēs trick you with a phony question.

Chapter fourteen

Were David and Jonathan gay?

Don't accuse someone of something they didn't do.
Jesus, Matthew 19:18

Our four main characters are –

- King Saul
- Saul's son, Jonathan
- Jonathan's son, Mephibosheth
- and David, a young shepherd from Bethlehem.

Yes, that David, of the famous David and Goliath. David was an Israelite and Goliath was a giant Philistine. The Philistines were Israel's enemy and their armies were about to face off in a battle. But when David killed Goliath, all the Philistines ran away. David's courageous act got the attention of king Saul. David still had Goliath's head in his hand when he was brought to meet Saul. Jonathan was there too.

I'll tell you the rest of the story by sharing a conversation –

Gāəthē – When Jonathan saw David it was love at first sight. The Bible says Jonathan's soul was knit with David's soul. It was so romantic.
1 Samuel 17:57; 18:1

Bəthē – There was nothing homosexual about Jonathan's soul being knit with David's soul. The same Hebrew words are used to say that Jacob's life was bound up in his son Benjamin's life.   Genesis 44:30

God didn't write the Old Testament to tell us stories about homosexual feelings. The Old Testament is about Jesus. God gave us a taste of what was to come by telling us about people who have a similarity to Jesus in some of their qualities and achievements. One of my favorites is what happened with Joseph and his brothers in Genesis chs. 37, 39-45.

Jonathan is not Jesus, but he has a resemblance to Jesus.

Gāəthē – Jonathan and David kissed.

Bəthē – You're thinking of 1 Samuel 20:41. It says David and Jonathan kissed each other and wept.

It wasn't romantic or sexual when men in the Bible kissed each other. When Esau saw his brother Jacob for the first time in twenty years, he ran to Jacob, hugged him, fell on his neck, and kissed him, and they wept. David and Jonathan were brothers too – brothers in arms. When Jonathan died, David said – my brother Jonathan.   Genesis 33:4; 2 Samuel 1:26

Gāəthē – Jonathan stripped himself of the robe he was wearing and gave it to David. He took off his robe so he could have sex with David.
1 Samuel 18:4

Bəthē – Jonathan was the king's son. He was royalty. Jonathan gave his royal robe to David to honor him for killing Israel's enemy, Goliath. The king of Persia, Ahasuerus, put his own royal clothing and crown on Mordecai to honor him for his good deed.   Esther 6:1-12

But there's more significance to the gift Jonathan gave to David. Here's the meaning of the robe. As the son of king Saul, Jonathan was next in line to the throne. But God anointed David to be king after Saul. When Jonathan took off his robe and gave it to David, Jonathan was stripping himself of his royalty and clothing David with it. That was a pattern, a picture of what Jesus would do for sinners.   1 Samuel 16:1,10-14

Jesus is royalty. He's the King. And Jesus became the Son of the King. He stripped Himself of His royalty so He could become a man and die for us and earn righteousness – salvation, for us. And Jesus gives His royal robe of righteousness to anyone who will give their life to Him.
Isaiah 33:22; Matthew 27:11

The robe that Jonathan gave to David represents God's righteousness.

> I will rejoice greatly in the Lord.
> My soul shall be joyful in my God.
> Because He has clothed me
> with the garments of salvation.
> He has covered me
> with the robe of righteousness.
> Isaiah 61:10

Gāəthē – David and Jonathan got married.

Bəthē – No, they didn't.

Gāəthē – Jonathan made a covenant with David. 1 Samuel 18:3

Bəthē – It wasn't unusual for two men to make a covenant. Abraham made a covenant with the Philistine king, Abimelech, so he could live in his country in peace. Genesis 21:25-34

Ask me another question and I'll tell you the meaning of the covenant Jonathan made with David.

Gāəthē – When Jonathan died, David adopted Jonathan's son, Mephibosheth. That's what same-sex couples do.

Bəthē – Mephibosheth was five years old when his father Jonathan, and his grandfather, king Saul, died in battle. 1 Samuel 31:6; 2 Samuel 1:11-12

As the grandson of the king, Saul's death was potentially a big problem for Mephibosheth. When Ahaziah, the king of Judah, died, his mother Athaliah had all of his sons killed so she could take the throne.
 2 Kings 11:1-3

Mephibosheth's nurse assumed the new king would kill Mephibosheth. So she picked him up and started running. But she ran so fast that Mephibosheth fell, and both of his feet became permanently injured. Because of that fall Mephibosheth was no longer able to walk.
 2 Samuel 4:4

Adam fell and became permanently injured spiritually when he ate from the tree. He took on a sinful nature that leads to death.

Because of the fall of that first man, all of us became unable to walk, spiritually. Do you think that's unfair? Why should you have to inherit sin and death? You didn't eat from the tree with Adam.

No, you didn't. But Jesus made the free gift of eternal life available to you even though you weren't nailed to a cross with Him.   Romans 5:12

> All of us who've been saved by Jesus
> will live forever because we
> made that connection with Him.
> It's similar to the way that all of us
> have to die because of our
> connection with Adam.
> 1 Corinthians 15:22

When king Saul died, David became king of Israel. And David told his people – see if there's anyone left alive of the house of Saul so I can show them the lovingkindness of God for Jonathan's sake. Now that David is king, he represents God the Father. Jonathan represents Jesus. And Mephibosheth is us – yes, you and me.   2 Samuel 9:1,3

David was told – yes, there's a son of Jonathan, named Mephibosheth, who's injured on both of his feet. So David sent men who brought Mephibosheth to him. That represents God sending His Holy Spirit to draw people to Him.   John 6:44

David showed the lovingkindness of God to Mephibosheth because of the covenant Jonathan made with David. That's a pure, holy love, the love that God feels. And it's a lesson about the lovingkindness that God shows to believers because of the covenant Jesus made.
   Hebrews 9:11-28

In the Old Testament, a covenant was sealed with the shedding of the blood of animals. God made a covenant with Abraham and He told Abraham to cut animals in pieces.   Genesis 15:7-21

Jesus made a covenant by shedding His own blood on a cross.

> Jesus blessed the bread.
> Then He broke it and gave it
> to the disciples, and said
> take, eat, this is My body.

> Then Jesus took the cup.
> He gave thanks and handed
> the cup to them, and said
> drink, all of you,
> because this is My blood
> of the new covenant, which is
> shed for as many as are willing,
> for the forgiveness of sins.
> Matthew 26:26-28

Jesus gave His life for us. And in the pattern, Jonathan gave his life in battle for Israel. David's faithfulness to the covenant that Jonathan made with him is an illustration of God's faithfulness to the covenant that Jesus made for us. 2 Samuel 1:12

> Oh give thanks to the Lord
> because He is good,
> and His mercy goes on forever.
> 1 Chronicles 16:34

Gāəthē – Jonathan loved David as his own soul. 1 Samuel 18:1,3

Bəthē – When Jonathan saw the way David killed Goliath, he knew David had the same faith in God that he had. That's why Jonathan loved David as his own soul.

Both David and Jonathan performed miraculous feats of bravery that could only be done by men who possessed an unusually great faith in God and who received the blessings of God. We see Jonathan's faith in his first words recorded in the Bible. Jonathan spotted an enemy encampment. The only one with him was his armorbearer. He said –

> We're going to attack the barracks
> of the idol worshipers.
> The Lord can give us the victory.
> He can win with two
> just as easily as He can with many.
> Jonathan, 1 Samuel 14:6

David's first words in the Bible were spoken after he heard Goliath taunt Israel's army. David said --

> I will teach this worshiper of dead idols
> that when he insults the armies of Israel,
> he's insulting the power of the living God.
> David, 1 Samuel 17:26

God gave the victory to both Jonathan and David.

Gāəthē – I've saved the best for last. Even a skeptic like you can't deny this final piece of biblical evidence. It proves beyond a doubt that Jonathan and David had a homosexual relationship.

When David was told that Jonathan died, he called Jonathan lovely and very pleasant. David tore his clothes, wept, fasted, and mourned. He wrote a poem about Jonathan and put it to music. And he told the people to learn it. David said – the beauty of Israel was slain.
2 Samuel 1:11-12,17-18; 2 Samuel 1:19,23,26 KJV

And David said this about Jonathan –

> Thy love to me was wonderful,
> Passing the love of women.
> David, 2 Samuel 1:26 KJV

Have you ever heard heterosexual men say their male friends loved them more than their own wives loved them?

Bəthē – Yes, I have. They're soldiers who've fought together in war. Men on the battlefield experience a bond that those of us who haven't been there don't know. They're willing to give their lives for each other. Jesus called it the greatest love –

> You who give your life so your
> friends can live – you are the ones
> who show the greatest love.
> Jesus, John 15:13

Soldiers have a love for each other that they don't have with their wives. Will you call them gay? Jesus said – love Me more than you love your wife. Will you say that's gay? Luke 14:26

David wasn't talking about a sexual or romantic love. He was talking about loyalty. Jonathan was the epitome of a loyal friend. David was loved by the people for his feats of bravery. But Jonathan never became jealous of David, like Saul did. 1 Samuel 18:5-16

Jonathan could have been king, but he gave way to David because David was God's choice for king. Jonathan's father tried to kill him for doing that, but Jonathan stayed faithful to David. Was it because he was gay for David? No. It was for the glory of God. Jonathan's love for David was a sacrificial love, like the love Jesus has for us.
1 Samuel 13:13-14; 16:13; 20:30-34; 22:7-8; 23:15-18

Jonathan was a pattern of Jesus, who loves His friends with a perfect loyalty. The apostle John was shown a vision of Jesus when He returns.

John said –

> I saw the One who is called
> Faithful and True.
> Revelation 19:11

Gāəthē – You can believe what you want. It's obvious to me that Jonathan and David had a sexual relationship.

Bəthē – Why do you say it's obvious?

Gāəthē – Because of the things they did to each other, and the things they said to each other and about each other. You haven't given any biblical evidence to prove that it wasn't sexual. You're trying to force your own opinion into the Bible.

Bəthē – My evidence is that the Bible never says they had sex.

You've accused Jonathan and David of a serious offense. In the nation of Israel, homosexuality was a crime punished by death.

> When a man has sexual intercourse
> with another man, as though that other man
> is a woman, then both of those men
> have done a disgusting thing that God hates.
> They are to be punished with death by execution.
> Their blood will be on them.
> Leviticus 20:13

But there must be witnesses.

> A person who commits a death penalty offense
> must only be put to death if there are
> two or three witnesses who will testify that they
> saw them committing the offense.
> Deuteronomy 17:6

The burden of proof is on you. The Bible says you must testify against Jonathan and David. And you have to throw the first stone at Jonathan and David's execution. Can you do that?

> The witnesses must start the execution.
> Deuteronomy 17:7

Did you see them having sex? No? Then on what do you base your accusation? On the righteous things they did to each other and said to and about each other? That's your evidence? Then you're a false witness. Do you realize the seriousness of what you've done? You've accused two good men of a death penalty offense without evidence.

Deuteronomy 19:16-21 says if someone makes false charges against a person, then they must receive the penalty for the crime they accused them of. You would have to take the death penalty that you tried to put on David and Jonathan.

Gāəthē – I'm not a false witness.

Bəthē – You are. And do you know what you're doing when you say David and Jonathan were gay?

Gāəthē – What?

Bəthē – You're crapping in your hand and wiping your crap on the pages of the Bible.

Chapter fifteen

Should you partake in a gay pride parade?

Instead of keeping their sin out of sight
– they made a parade of it!
Look at them. They have no shame.
They're just like Sodom.
Woe to them.
They've rewarded themselves with evil.
                    God, Isaiah 3:9

Incredibly evil things have been done to gay people. So you march in gay pride parades to say – we will no longer be treated like we were in the past. We want to live freely, without being tortured. We'll fight for it, and march with pride.

But God doesn't want to see you parading down the street celebrating your sin. He hates that kind of pride. God wants you to have a broken spirit over your sin.

> You're proud of things
> you should be ashamed of.
> Philippians 3:19

If you march in a gay pride parade or cheer along on the sidelines, you're committing an act of arrogance against God. The Bible says arrogance leads to destruction.

> If you lift yourself up too high
> you'll fall and break all your bones.
> Proverbs 16:18

God sees your gay pride parade as idolatry. You've rejected Him, made yourself a god, and created your own law. Gay pride adds sin to sin.

> Were you ashamed when
> you committed abomination?
> No. You weren't ashamed at all.
> You don't even know how to blush.
> Therefore you will fall among them that fall.
> You will be cast down
> at the time that I visit you.
> God, Jeremiah 6:15

Gay pride is not the way to deal with the cruelty and horror you were subjected to in the past. Jesus Christ is the way. The right response is to repent of the sin of homsx and turn to Jesus.

You're doing a terrible thing to gay people when you applaud at a gay pride parade. It's not love at all.

> You know that God will sentence to death
> those who practice things like homosexuality.
> But you do them anyway,
> and applaud others who do them.
> Romans 1:32

If you applaud at a gay pride parade, then God will hold you guilty for the sin of homsx – even if you don't do homsx.

> All of you will be damned,
> who refuse to believe the truth
> and take pleasure in wrongdoing.
> 2 Thessalonians 2:12

There are gay pride parades and parades to honor championship sports teams. But few people appreciate what Jesus did by going to the cross to suffer and die for us. One day there will be the greatest parade ever – when Jesus returns on a horse with His army following Him. Jesus will have so many in His army, it will look like that parade will go on forever. No one will be able to ignore Jesus then.

You have two choices. If you march in gay pride parades then Jesus won't let you ride with Him in His parade. Which do you want?
Revelation 19:11-14; 21:8

> Don't delight in evil things.
> Delight in the truth.
> 1 Corinthians 13:6

Chapter sixteen

Where's Paul of the Gāəthēs?

Paul of the Gāəthēs said –

> The Holy Spirit has given us clear and sufficient warnings,
> that from the time our Lord Jesus walked the earth,
> until the time He returns – there will be people
> infiltrating the Church.
>
> The devil has his own disciples
> working inside the Church. They reject true teachings, and let evil
> spirit-beings use them to spread the devil's teachings.
>
> They say gay people can't get married.
> And they say no one can eat pork – a food God created to be
> eaten by those who believe in Him – by those who know the truth
> and appreciate God's gift of pork.
>
> They speak those lies while pretending to be Christians.
> It's like they pressed hot metal against their sense of
> right and wrong until there was no feeling left.
>
> The Bible says everything God created is holy and good
> and is to be received with thanksgiving.
> So say your prayers and eat your pork.
> And enjoy your holy homosexuality.
>
> Paul of the Gāəthēs, 1 Timothy 4:1-5 GRV
> Gāəthē Revised Version of the Bible

Bəthē thinks he might have spotted him in Harvard Square –

Bəthē – Excuse me. Paul? Paul of the Gāəthēs?

PatG – Yes.

Bəthē – My name is Bəthē.

PatG – Oh, Bəthē. I've heard of you.

Bəthē – You have?

PatG – From PetG.

Bəthē – Do you have time to talk?

PatG – Sure.

Bəthē – Shall we go to the Coop?

PatG – Okay.

Bəthē – I had a classmate in fifth grade named Paul of the Gāəthēs.

PatG – You did?

Bəthē – No. Do you go by PatG?

PatG – That's fine.

Bəthē – The G at the end makes it sound like you're from India.

PatG – I've been told that.

Bəthē – You've done a bad thing with 1 Timothy 4:1-5.

PatG – What did I get wrong?

Bəthē – Everything.

PatG – That bad?

Bəthē – It's serious, PatG.

PatG – Okay Bəthē, let me have it.

Bəthē – It has nothing to do with homosexuality or pork.

PatG – Verse 4 says everything God created is good.

Bəthē – Yes, God saw that everything He made was very good.

Genesis 1:31

PatG – So, what's the problem?

Bəthē – A thing is good as long as you use it correctly.

PatG – What are pigs good for?

Bəthē – Eating filth.

PatG – First Timothy 4:5 say homosexuality and pork are made holy when you pray over them.

Bəthē – No, it doesn't. Praying over your pork won't make it edible.

PatG – Are you disagreeing with the Word of God?

Bəthē – No, PatG. But you've found the answer.

PatG – I did?

Bəthē – Who is Paul talking about in this passage?

PatG – Who?

Bəthē – Verse one says it's – some (KJV.)

PatG – Some who?

Bəthē – Some who depart from the faith.

PatG – What's the faith?

Bəthē – The faith here means the true teachings – God's Word.

PatG – Okay.

Bəthē – Some listened to teachings from demons.

PatG – Right, teachings that banned homosexuality and pork.

Bəthē – No. Those aren't teachings from demons.

PatG – Who's teachings are they?

Bəthē – God's teachings. God banned homosexuality and pork.

PatG – No, Bəthē. Verse three says God created homosexuality and pork to be received with thanksgiving by those who know the truth.

Bəthē – It doesn't say that, PatG. God didn't make homosexuality at all, and He didn't make pork to be eaten by humans.   Leviticus 11:7; 20:13

PatG – Alright. Tell me Bəthē. What's this passage about?

Bəthē – It's about the leader of a Christian cult who tells their followers that Jesus will reject them on Judgment Day if they're not vegetarians. Jesus never said that. That's why Paul calls it a teaching from devils.

It's about a Christian cult that won't let its priests get married. God does not forbid His priests from marrying – in a heterosexual marriage. The false teachers were forbidding things that God said were good. They said you can't have a heterosexual marriage. They said you can't eat the foods that God said you can eat.   Isaiah 5:20

People who call themselves Christians but don't have God's Holy Spirit create Christian cults and oppress people with teachings that come from the devil and his demons. God's laws are not doctrines of devils. Will you consider these things?

PatG – You've certainly given me food for thought.

Bəthē – People's spiritual lives are at stake. And so is yours.

More PatG in the GRV –

> All of us who believe in Jesus
> are children of God.
> We're all one.
> We're not slave or free,
> Jew or Greek,
> gay or straight,
> male or female,
> up or down,
> right or wrong,
> wet or dry,
> decaf or regular.
>
> We're not one thing or the other.
> Not saint or sinner,
> drunk or sober,
> those who have
> sexual intercourse with animals
> or those who don't,
> those who repent
> or those who don't,
> those who obey Jesus,
> or those who don't.
>
> Paul of the Gāəthēs, Galatians 3:27-28 GRV
> Gāəthē Revised Version of the Bible

Paul of the Gāəthēs adds what God subtracts. People who don't have God's Holy Spirit use bad math.

Chapter seventeen

Why can't you be Gay Christian?

I testify to everyone who hears
the teachings that are written in the Bible.

If you add to those teachings,
then God will add to you the punishments
that are written about in the Bible.

And if you take away from
those teachings, then God will
take you away from the Tree of Life
and away from the Holy City
that are written about in the Bible.
                Revelation 22:18-19

You can't be –

- Liar Christian
- Tarot card Christian
- Pot-smoker Christian
- Masturbator Christian
- Abortionist Christian
- Racist Christian
- Shoplifter Christian
- Alcoholic Christian

So why would anyone think they can be Gay Christian?

Gay Christian is breaking the third commandment –

> Don't attach God's name to a lie.
> Exodus 20:7

Gay Christian is a porneia Christian. You can't be that.

> Christians must never
> be named Porneia Christian.
> Ephesians 5:3

> Run from porneia like you're
> escaping from a burning building.
> 1 Corinthians 6:18

When you're born a second time, you're not gay anymore.   John 3:3

> When you're joined to Christ, you're a
> new creation. The old things pass away,
> and behold, you're a new person.
> 2 Corinthians 5:17

Gay Christian can't say he's received Jesus as his Lord and Savior. Before you can say that, you have to say gay is sin. Gay and Christian cancel each other out. They're morally inconsistent.

> Jesus doesn't sing harmony
> with the devil.
> 2 Corinthians 6:15

> We who died to the sin life
> can no longer spend our life in sin.
> Romans 6:2

> Be holy because I am holy.
> God, Leviticus 11:44; 19:2

Gay Christian might say he believes in Jesus, or tell you he's been going to church since he was a child, or talk about how much he respects the authority of the Bible. But by calling himself Gay Christian he reveals the truth – he's been window shopping with no intention to buy.

> Why do you call Me Lord, Lord,
> but don't do what I say?
> Jesus, Luke 6:46

Gay Christian is practicing sin.

> If you practice sin, you're of the devil.
> 1 John 3:8

> Truly, truly, I say to you – if you practice sin,
> you're not free. You're the servant of sin.
> But if I set you free,
> you'll know what freedom is.
> Jesus, John 8:34,36

> Let everyone who names the name
> of Christ depart from sin.
> 2 Timothy 2:19

Chapter eighteen

Were Ruth and Naomi gay?

Oh Lord, my Rock,
and my Redeemer.
          Psalm 19:14

Here's Bəthē, and a new character, Ms. Gāəthē –

Ms. Gāəthē – You guys are hypocrites.

Bəthē – Why do you say that?

Ms. Gāəthē – You call us sinners, and then you use our wedding vows.

Bəthē – What wedding vows?

Ms. Gāəthē – The ones Ruth made to Naomi.

Bəthē – They didn't get married. Ruth was Naomi's daughter-in-law. That would be incest and homosexuality. Ruth and Naomi reverenced God and His laws.   Leviticus 18:15; Romans 1:26

Ms. Gāəthē – God put the book of Ruth in the Bible to show us the love, beauty, and loyalty of Ruth's lesbian relationship with Naomi.

Bəthē – No. God put the book of Ruth in the Bible to show us the love, beauty, and loyalty of Ruth's relationship with her husband Boaz. Why? Because their relationship bears a likeness to the relationship Jesus Christ has with those He redeems by His sacrificial death.

Ms. Gāəthē – God blessed the marriage of Ruth and Naomi.

Bəthē – What makes you say that?

Ms. Gāəthē – In Genesis 2:24, God said a man cleaves to his wife. Then He used the same Hebrew word to say Ruth cleaved to Naomi. That's when Ruth made her wedding vows to Naomi. She said – where you go, I will go – where you live, I will live – where you die, I will die.
                                                        Ruth 1:14,16-17

Bəthē – You're defeating your argument by using Genesis 2:24. That's where God said marriage is for a man and a woman. And the word cleave is also used for loyalty. King Hezekiah cleaved to the Lord when he showed his loyalty to the Lord by obeying Him.   2 Kings 18:6

Here's what really happened. There was a famine in Israel. So Naomi and her husband Elimelech, and their two sons, left Israel and moved to Moab. Naomi's sons married Moabite women – Ruth and Orpah. But then Naomi's husband, and her two sons, all died in Moab.

Naomi heard there was food again in Israel. So she decided to return to Israel by herself. She told Ruth and Orpah to move back in with their mothers in Moab. Orpah did as Naomi said. And Naomi told Ruth that Orpah went back to her people and to her gods. Ruth 1:15

Ruth didn't go home to her mother like Orpah did. Ruth didn't return to the gods of Moab, the dead idols made of stone. Jesus said if you want to become His disciple you must love Him more than you love your father, mother, spouse, children, and your own life. Luke 14:26

You left out something that Ruth told Naomi. She said – your God will be my God. Ruth 1:16

Ruth loved Naomi because Naomi was her mother-in-law. But Ruth had a greater love. She had an intense desire to be loyal to, and obey Naomi's God. When Ruth cleaved to Naomi, she was cleaving to the one true living God. Ruth wasn't making wedding vows to Naomi. The vows Ruth made were to God.

Ms. Gāəthē – You're blinded by your prejudice. You're okay with two women having a close relationship – but if you find out they're lovers, then you object.

Bəthē – The Bible never says Ruth and Naomi were lovers or gay.

Ms. Gāəthē – That was to protect them from hateful bigots. We saw the same thing in our own recent history. Lesbian couples lived together but had to keep their sexuality a secret. It was called a Boston marriage.

In her wedding vows to Naomi, Ruth said – till death do us part. She knew they could be killed for being in a lesbian marriage. In Ruth and Naomi's time women were not permitted to live on their own. They were punished if they didn't marry a man.

Ruth had to go out to the fields and pick up food that was left on the ground so she and Naomi could eat.

Bəthē – Ruth knew she needed to be saved from her hunger for food. God led her to the field owned by Boaz. When you know you need to be saved from your sin, then God will lead you to Jesus. Boaz was to Ruth as Jesus is to sinners.   Ruth 2:3; Luke 19:1-10; John 6:44

Ms. Gāəthē – Boaz didn't love Ruth.

Bəthē – Boaz was a God-fearing man. He greeted his workers by saying – the Lord be with you. And they responded – the Lord bless you. Boaz saw Ruth lawfully gleaning food in his field – and he told her not to go to another field. Boaz encouraged Ruth by telling her that he instructed his workers to let her take what she needs.   Leviticus 23:22

Ruth couldn't understand why Boaz was kind to her, since she was a foreigner. Boaz told Ruth he admired her because of what she did for Naomi. Ruth was from Moab, but she took care of Naomi, an Israelite.

Jesus said – I was hungry and you gave Me something to eat. When? When you gave something to eat to even the most lowly of My people. Ruth obeyed Jesus over a thousand years before Jesus was born.
                                                                    Matthew 25:35

Boaz loved Ruth with a holy love. He admired Ruth because of the reason why she left the country where she was born and came to a place she didn't know. Boaz told Ruth – may the Lord repay you for what you've done. May the Lord give you a full reward – because you've run to the shelter of His wings of protection.   Ruth 2:10-12

Ms. Gāəthē – Ruth didn't love Boaz.

Bəthē – The love Ruth had for Boaz was the best love. God's Holy Spirit put Ruth's love for Boaz in her heart. It was given to her as a reward for her desire to obey God.   Acts 5:32

Ruth responded to the kindness that Boaz showed her by bowing herself to the ground. Ruth was humble. The kindness Boaz showed to Ruth was a pattern of the kindness that Jesus shows to the humble.

> Happy are those who have a humble spirit.
> Jesus, Matthew 5:3

Ruth and Boaz showed each other love and respect. They had a wonderful romance that had a spiritual foundation.

Ms. Gāəthē – Naomi told Ruth to stay in the field owned by Boaz because Boaz gave Ruth a lot of food. Naomi wanted more food.

Bəthē – When Ruth went home and told Naomi she was working in the field owned by Boaz, Naomi said – I pray that the Lord blesses Boaz.

Naomi praised God for showing them His lovingkindness. It wasn't for food that Naomi told Ruth to stay in the field owned by Boaz. She told Ruth that Boaz was a kinsman, and one of their redeemers. Boaz was of the same family as Naomi's husband, Elimelech.   Ruth 2:3

A redeemer is someone who pays a price to free another person. God made laws in Israel that there be kinsman redeemers who could redeem a relative from slavery.   Leviticus 25:47-49; Ruth 2:20

And God said if a woman's husband dies and they had no son, then her husband's – nearest unmarried male relative – is to marry her. And he is to have a son with her. That son will be the son of her husband who died, and will carry on her husband's name.   Deuteronomy 25:5-10

Ms. Gāəthē – Naomi told Ruth to marry Boaz.

Bəthē – Naomi told Ruth – I will seek rest for you. Jesus said if you team up with Him, you'll find rest for your soul. Hebrews 4:9 says we who believe in Jesus enter into that rest.   Ruth 3:1; Matthew 11:29

Naomi told Ruth to go at midnight, to the place where Boaz was sleeping and lie down at his feet. Ruth did as Naomi said. When Boaz was startled by her presence, she said – it's me, Ruth, your servant.

Ruth asked Boaz to spread the corner of his coat over her because he's her near kinsman. The word coat can mean a wing. Ruth was asking Boaz to marry her and spread his wing of protection over her. That's a pattern of when God told the people of Israel that He spread the corner of His garment over them. Ruth 3:9; Ezekiel 16:8

When Ruth asked Boaz to spread his coat over her, it was symbolic of a believer running to God's protection.

Boaz told Ruth he will perform the role of kinsman redeemer for her. But, he said, there's a kinsman nearer to her. So, the next day, in front of ten witnesses, in a public place, Boaz asked the nearer kinsman if he would redeem Ruth. But he said no. He wouldn't pay the price and make the sacrifice involved in redeeming Ruth. So Boaz redeemed her. That was a picture of how Jesus redeems sinners.

> Jesus did not come to earth to be served.
> He came to serve. He gave His life
> to pay the ransom price. Jesus gave
> His one life to redeem many sinners.
> Mark 10:45

> But now, through Christ Jesus,
> you who were once far away, are now close by
> because Christ shed His blood for you
> when He died on a cross.
> Ephesians 2:13

Those who seek to know the true God, are redeemed by Jesus, our Kinsman Redeemer. Jesus paid the price in full. Jesus paid with His blood, with His life to buy us. Colossians 1:12-14; Hebrews 9:12; 1 Peter 1:18-21; Revelation 5:4-9

> In Whom we have redemption
> through His blood,
> the forgiveness of sins.
> Ephesians 1:7 KJV

Ms. Gāəthē – Boaz bought Ruth like she was a thing. That's not love.

Bəthē – It's the best love. Ruth and Boaz married in obedience to God. They obeyed God's law of the kinsman redeemer. That's a pattern of those of us who obey the Gospel of Jesus Christ and receive the redemption of our souls and eternal life. Romans 1:5; 16:26

The marriage of Boaz and Ruth is a pattern of the marriage of Jesus and His wife, those who've obediently given their lives to Him.
Matthew 25:1-13;
Ephesians 5:32; Revelation 19:7-9

Ms. Gāəthē – You don't see the truth because you can't handle the fact that God devoted a book of the Bible to two women in love.

Bəthē – You've slandered Ruth and Naomi. And you've made evil claims about God. You would be wise to ask God to forgive you.

Chapter nineteen

Are two men as good as a man and a woman?

Why don't you read the Bible?
In Genesis 1:27, 2:21-24, and 5:2,
God said that from the beginning
He created marriage to be
between a male and a female.
        Jesus, Matthew 19:4-6

Gāəthēs say that when God created the first marriage between a man and a woman, He didn't explicitly state that He won't accept smsx marriages. So, when Bəthēs say God won't accept smsx marriages, gāəthēs accuse us of adding something to the Bible that's not there.

Gāəthēs are adding something that's not there – smsx marriages.

God said He will kill anyone who attempts to create a marriage with two men. There's your explicit statement.   Leviticus 20:13

Then the gāəthēs say – no, it's in the text of Genesis that God never explicitly states that He won't accept a marriage between two men. Okay, let's see what the text says.

God created Adam first, and then God said –

> It is not good that the man should be alone;
> I will make him an help meet for him.
> God, Genesis 2:18 KJV

The words – an help meet for him – are the Hebrew words 5828 and 5048 in the Strong's Concordance. Those words say that God made Eve to be Adam's opposite – his counterpart. A study of the text shows why God did not create a man for Adam to marry.

God said marriage is to be between two people with opposite bodies. To hold something together you need a bolt and a screw, two opposite parts – the part and the counterpart, or the mate, as some call it.

There's your explicit statement in the text. God told Adam and Eve to help themselves to the complementary genitalia.

God said – I'm giving you guys penises. You'll want to stick them in something. That's good. I've given you the woman's vagina for that. You can stick your penis in your wife's vagina all you want. Just make sure you let her know first. Enjoy.   1 Corinthians 7:3-5

And God said – now, at some point you might get the idea of sticking your penis in a man's mouth or anus. Don't do that. I hate it when you do that. I've arranged it so that you'll get painful and sometimes fatal diseases if you do that. Stop doing that. If you refuse to stop, and laugh in My face, then I'll kill you in hell.   Deuteronomy 28:22; 58-61

God tells gay people – you refused to obey the conscience I put in your mind, you refused to obey the Bible I gave you – you refused to learn from the diseases I gave you and from what I did to Sodom. At a certain point it will be too late. Repent now.
     Romans 1:18-20; 2:11-16

God created two sexes and one marriage. That's it. Homsx is a use of the human body that God never intended.

Chapter twenty

Should a man look like a woman?

Bəthē – Paul said homosexuality is unnatural. Romans 1:26-27

Gāəthē – He also said long hair on a man is unnatural.
1 Corinthians 11:14

Bəthē – What's your point?

Gāəthē – Homosexuality isn't sinful.

Bəthē – Why did Paul call it unnatural?

Gāəthē – Because in the culture of Paul's day, women were seen as weak and inferior. So, the receptive partner in a homosexual act was called unnatural because he was acting like a woman. You know, in some of his writings Paul sounds like a misogynist. But compared to the men of his day, he was quite the little suffragist.

Bəthē – No. Paul got his teachings from the Old Testament –

> Females must never be dressed up
> in that which males wear.
> And males are never to be arrayed
> in that which females wear.
> Because all who do those things
> are an abomination
> to the Lord your God.
> Deuteronomy 22:5

The reason Paul wrote 1 Corinthians 11:1-16 is because the church at Corinth was blurring the distinctions between male and female.

Gāəthē – How do you know what those distinctions are?

Bəthē – Paul said you know it when you see it –

> We know instinctively that long hair
> on a man is disgraceful.
> 1 Corinthians 11:14

It's pleasing when you see a woman with flowers in her hair, it feels right. But when you see a man with flowers in his hair, you know it's wrong. You know that earrings, hair buns, bracelets, and pocketbooks don't belong on a man. But they look natural, proper, and lovely on a woman. You know it's wrong when you see a woman with a man's haircut and men's clothing.

Paul's teaching the same thing in 1 Corinthians 11:1-16 that he taught in Romans 1:26-27. God wants men to look and act like men – and women to look and act like women. If you saw Adam and Eve in the Garden of Eden, you'd see that their bodies looked different. Adam had the penis, and Eve had the vagina and breasts.

God's law in the Bible – and nature – make it clear that the place where a penis goes is in a vagina. When you stick your penis in a man, you're poking your finger in God's eye. And He doesn't like that.

God's law forbids homosexuality, cross-dressing, transsexualism, gender-free, transvestism, uni-sex, transgenderism – and anything else that blurs the distinctions between men and women. God wants a clear difference between men and women. He wants different hair – long for women, and short for men. When you look at someone you should know immediately which sex they are.

It's a sin against God to call a man "she," or to call a woman "he." It's against God's law to have males in female's bathrooms and locker rooms, or to have females in male's bathrooms and locker rooms.

If you were born with a penis, then God does not want you to compete in female's sporting events. God wants you to dress and act like a boy and then a man. If you were born with a vagina, then God wants you to dress and act like a girl and then a woman.

Gāəthē – I've got you now Bəthē. God said a man who takes the vow of a Nazirite must let his hair grow and not cut it. That vow could last for years, or, as in the case of Samson, for his entire life   Numbers 6:5; Judges 13:7

And 2 Samuel 14:25-26 says king David's son, Absalom, was the most beautiful man in Israel – and he only cut his hair once a year. And the prophet Elisha was mocked because he was bald. So, it's not always unnatural for a man to have long hair. 2 Kings 2:23

Bəthē – God ordered Nazirites to have long hair – and only them. It was an exception – like when God made an exception for priests – and only them, to work on the sabbath. Numbers 28:9-10;
See Exodus 20:8-11; Numbers 15:32-36

And you're being dishonest about Absalom's hair. The Bible just makes mention of it. It doesn't say God approved of his long hair. Absalom was not a Nazirite. Second Samuel 14:25 says it was the people who praised Absalom for his beauty – not God.

Absalom was no hero. Second Samuel 15:6 says he used deception to gain the people's loyalty and affection. He tried to steal the throne away from his father, king David. That made Absalom a pattern of the antichrist, who will try to take the place of Jesus. 2 Samuel 15:10-14
2 Thessalonians 2:3-4;
1 John 2:18; Revelation 13:11-18

And in 2 Kings 2:23 some boys called Elisha bald head. But what they mocked was not Elisha's baldness. They mocked the miracle that God had just done by carrying Elisha's mentor, Elijah, to Heaven in a whirlwind. They mocked God. 2 Kings 2:11

So, you're wrong. God's standards don't change. And everyone knows those standards. Paul taught them from the Old Testament. And people who don't have the written Word have the law written in their heart. They learn by observing nature and from their conscience. They know instinctively, or as Romans 2:14 says – by nature.
Romans 1:20; 2:14-15

Gāəthē – My church fights for transgender rights.

Bəthē – I know. The first thing people see at your church is a huge trans flag right there by the front door. You've replaced the cross of Christ with a flag that celebrates sin.

You're saying – Christianity is about being proud of your sin. You're mocking God by bringing the world into the church instead of the church into the world. But you will reap what you sow.

Galatians 6:7

Gāəthē – There's a cross out front too

Bəthē – Right, your church's flag has a cross on it. But you've changed the meaning of the cross. The message of the cross is – receive salvation and live eternally by repenting of your sin and giving your life to Jesus because He died for you.

Gāəthē – We're just showing love to our fellow human beings

Bəthē – That's what you call love? You're encouraging people to mutilate bodies that were made in the image of God.   James 3:9

Gāəthē – We want to speak up for oppressed people.

Bəthē – Then why don't you have a flag for the girls who are raped because they're Christians? Why don't you have a flag for the Christians whose arms are hacked off two inches at a time to try and get them to stop following Christ?

Christians are the most persecuted people in the world – and it's not even close. Christians around the world, including children, are relentlessly persecuted in the most horrifying ways. They have everything taken from them – their right to religion and speech, their jobs, homes and children. They're imprisoned, tortured, raped, burned to death, and crucified. Why do so-called Christian churches have flags out front for gay and trans but not for them?

Gāəthē – Trans people are heroes.

Bəthē – No, It's not heroic to be trans. Heroic is firefighters and police officers running into the burning World Trade Center. The heros are the members of the military, law enforcement, and firefighters – and all those who put their lives on the line every day to serve and protect us.

The heros are those who fight, suffer unimaginably, and die in wars so we can live free. Real heros are being ignored. What about disabled veterans, and members of the military and law enforcement who gave their lives protecting the rest of us? When will we see them in TV ads for banks and clothing companies?

Trans people might do heroic things but being trans is not heroic. Trans is something to be ashamed of and repented of.

Gāəthē – We want to protect trans people's rights.

Bəthē – Why don't you care about protecting the rights of Christians?

A Christian schoolteacher can be fired for obeying God by refusing to use the required pronouns.

Transgenders are let into schools to influence young children, but Christians and the Bible are banned from schools.

Universities are stripping female athletes of their right to decency by forcing them to share a locker room with exposed penises. And if the female athletes speak up about it, they face retaliation. They could be denied employment. This is the next step in the degeneration.

2 Timothy 3:1-5, 12-13

Children are taught to celebrate trans and disrespect police officers.

Romans 13:1-7

In 2021, the U.S. State Department started flying rainbow pride flags with the the American flag. The government has made gay and trans rights a top priority. Meanwhile, our enemies plot our destruction. The nation that flies pride flags with their flag will be punished by God.

Leviticus 18:24-28; Psalms 33:12

Chapter twenty-one

Did Jesus heal a man's male lover?

In Matthew 8:5-13 and Luke 7:1-10 we're told about an encounter Jesus had with a centurion – an officer in the Roman army who was in charge of a hundred soldiers.

The centurion went to Jesus with an emergency –

> Lord, my servant is at my house, in bad shape.
> He's paralyzed and unable to get out of bed.
> It's torturing him. And Lord, he's going to die.
> Matthew 8:6

Jesus replied –

> I'll come and heal him.
> Matthew 8:7

Let's listen in again on a conversation between Gāəthē and Bəthē –

Gāəthē – Jesus approved of a homosexual relationship.

Bəthē – He never did that.

Gāəthē – He healed a centurion's male lover.

Bəthē – Why do you say they were lovers?

Gāəthē – The servant was dear to the centurion.   Luke 7:2 KJV

Bəthē – In the original Greek, the word dear is entimos. It appears five other times in the New Testament, and always refers to people who are exceptionally good and honorable. The apostle Peter wrote that Jesus is entimos, or precious, as the KJV translates it.   Luke 14:8; 1 Peter 2:4,6

The centurion said that when he tells his servant to do something, he does it. That would make a servant entimos.   Luke 7:8

Gāəthē – Maybe so. But the word Matthew and Luke used for servant is the Greek word pais.   Matthew 8:6,8,13; Luke 7:7

To understand what the writers of the Bible are teaching, we have to study the words they used. We do that by finding out how those words were used in the culture and languages of the world at the time.

When Matthew and Luke wrote their Gospel accounts, Greek writers were using the word pais to refer to a younger man who was in a homosexual relationship with an older man.

Jesus would not have been ignorant of what the word pais meant. If you put aside your prejudices, you'll be able to see the clear teaching of the Word of God. When Jesus healed the centurion's pais, Jesus was showing us that He blesses homosexual relationships.

Bəthē – The reason you're wrong is that you don't know the Bible or the power of God.   Matthew 22:29

If I take my Strong's Concordance and look up the word servant that was used by the centurion in Matthew 8:6, I see that it's # 3816. And the Greek dictionary in the back of the Strong's tells me it's the word pais.

I have a book called the New Englishman's Greek-English Concordance & Lexicon, by Wigram-Green. It uses the numbers from the Strong's Concordance. In that book I can look up # 3816 and see every verse where the word pais appears in the New Testament.

For instance, when Jesus was twelve years old, Luke called Jesus the Child. The word Luke used for Child is pais. Years later, Jesus took the hand of a girl who had died, and Jesus said – maid, arise. The word maid is pais. She rose from the dead and Jesus said – feed her.
                                                                           Luke 2:43; 8:54 KJV

You don't know the Bible
Yes, there are several in the Bible who are called pais. But do you know who's not called pais? Homosexuals. In the Bible, the word pais never means a homosexual. And it never has anything to do with any kind of sexual relationship.

And you don't know the power of God

> God takes words that the world uses.
> And He heats them in an oven seven times,
> until those words are like pure silver.
> Therefore, the words of the Lord are clean words.
> Psalm 12:6

That's why God can use a word like pais, a word that was used in an evil way by the people of the world. That's the power of God.

In John 1:1, Jesus is called the Word. The word John used to call Jesus the Word, is the Greek word logos. At the same time as John was writing his Gospel account, Greek writers were also using the word logos. They said the logos was a force that emanated from God and moved in the world.

If you interpreted the word logos using the same method that you interpreted pais, then you would come to an incorrect conclusion. You would think Jesus was a force that emanated from God. When we study the Bible we see that Jesus is God Himself in a human body. Jesus is the eternal God, the Creator. God took the word logos and gave it an entirely different meaning.

You're making a fatal error when you interpret words in the Bible according to the way the world uses those words. If you want the truth, then you need to let the Bible interpret itself.

It doesn't matter if the people of the world used the word pais to mean a man's boy lover. What matters is how God used it in the Bible.

Gāəthēs make everything dirty.

Gāəthē – You refuse to see what the Bible says because of your prejudice against gay people. You're saying Jesus would refuse to heal someone because they're in a homosexual relationship. You're calling Jesus a bigot.

Bəthē – No. I'm sure Jesus healed gay people. The Bible says He healed multitudes. There would have been gays and straights. They were liars, thieves, and murderers – and people engaged in all kinds of sexual immorality. Matthew 12:15; 14:14; 19:2

But when Jesus healed their physical illnesses it did not mean He approved of the sinful things they were doing. Jesus healed them because of the love and compassion He felt for them. And the healings were a sign. It was to let the people know that He is the One who can heal them of their sin sickness. Isaiah 35:5-6; Acts 2:22

Having your physical body healed by Jesus does not save your soul.

And having your soul saved by Jesus does not heal your physical body.

There's no evidence that the pais was the centurion's lover. But, for the sake of argument, what if he was? Would Jesus have healed the pais? Maybe. But if Jesus did heal him, He would not do it without warning the centurion to repent. Jesus would tell the centurion to stop having sex with his servant and treat him decently.

There was a man who had been sick for thirty-eight years. Jesus healed the man, and said to him – look, I've made you healthy – now sin no more or something worse will happen to you. John 5:14

Because of His love for us, Jesus died for the sins of the whole world. Gays too. But the compassion of Jesus won't get you to Heaven. You have to do your part by repenting and turning from your sins.
Acts 3:19; 1 John 2:2

> Repent.
> Jesus, Matthew 4:17

A group of ten lepers asked Jesus to heal them. And He healed them. One of the ten yelled out – glory to God! Then he fell down on his face at the feet of Jesus. And Jesus said to him – rise up, your faith has saved you. The other nine got their bodies healed. Only the one who went to Jesus and worshiped Him got his soul saved. Luke 17:11-19

But the centurion and his pais were not in a homosexual relationship. The centurion was a good man.

Gāəthē – You don't want to admit that God put this in the Bible to show us that He has no problem with homosexuality.

Bəthē – No. It's in the Bible as an illustration that there's only one way to be saved, and no other. Those who think they're saved because of any reason other than faith in Jesus are lost.

The centurion said to Jesus –

> Lord, I'm not good enough
> for You to enter my house.
> I know that if You just say the word,
> then my servant will be healed.
> Matthew 8:8

Jesus marvelled at the man's faith. He said to His followers –

> I haven't been able to find such great faith as this.
> Not even among My own people.
> Jesus, Matthew 8:10

Some of His followers looked down on those who weren't part of their group. Jesus taught them that He welcomes anyone who will believe in Him. It doesn't matter if they're a Roman centurion.   Luke 9:49-56

And Jesus said to the Centurion –

> Go on home now.
> And as much as you have believed,
> that's how much will be done for you.
> Jesus, Matthew 8:13

When the Centurion got home he found his servant healed.

Does that mean Jesus will heal anyone who asks? No. We're promised the salvation of our souls through our faith. We're not promised the healing of our bodies. God heals or doesn't heal according to His purposes. God might heal you or He might not. Your illness might be the thing that leads you to repentance and salvation. Or it might be what leads someone else to salvation. John 3:16

God might not heal your illness for your spiritual good. Your soul is what matters.

You've taken a beautiful story of saving faith and used it as an excuse to sin. Jesus came to save sinners, not to affirm people in their sins. You've slandered the Holy One, Jesus.

The lesson in the encounter with the centurion is that Jesus will save the soul of anyone who has genuine faith in Him.

Gāəthē – My point exactly. Jesus doesn't care about who a person chooses to love. He cares about their faith.

Bəthē – Jesus would not commend the faith of someone who was in a homosexual relationship.

Chapter twenty-two

What's Sodom?

> Two angels came to Sodom at sunset.
> Lot was sitting at the gate to Sodom,
> and he greeted the angels respectfully.
>
> Lot urged the angels to spend the night
> at his house. The angels said – no,
> we'll spend the night on the street.
> But Lot pleaded with them.
> And they said okay. So, Lot took them
> to his house and fed them dinner.
>
> But just as they were about to go to sleep,
> the men of Sodom surrounded Lot's house.
> They were young and old men,
> from all over Sodom.
>
> They called out to Lot and said – where are
> the men? Bring them out here so we can
> <u>know</u> them. But Lot said to them – I beg you,
> don't do such a wicked thing...
>
> The angels said to Lot – we will destroy
> this place...Then the Lord rained down fire
> and brimstone on Sodom...
>   Genesis 19:1-7,13,24

The men told Lot they wanted to <u>know</u> the angels. Some say – we don't know what they meant, maybe they didn't want sex, maybe they just wanted to get to know the angels. And yes, it is true that the word <u>know</u> (# 3045 in the Hebrew dictionary in the Strong's Concordance) can mean to get to know someone.

But it can also mean to have sex. Genesis 4:1 says Adam <u>knew</u> his wife, and she became pregnant. Adam and Eve did more than get to know each other. How do we know what the men of Sodom meant by know? Context. Lot told them not to do such a wicked thing. It's not a wicked thing to want to get to know someone. And God doesn't kill people for being friendly. The Bible makes it clear what the men of Sodom did.

In the first book of the Bible, God showed us what He does to people who won't stop showing Him their butthole. Sodom is a miniature hell. It's the model for the hell in the last book of the Bible –

> If your name's not written in the book of life,
> then you'll be thrown into the lake of fire.
> Revelation 20:15

Sodom is a warning –

> God passed sentence on the people of Sodom.
> He used a catastrophe to execute them.
> God incinerated them and turned them to ashes.
> He made sure that everyone would know what He did to them. Sodom stands as an example of what happens to people who want to live a wicked life.
> 2 Peter 2:6

In Luke 17:28-30, Jesus said that when He returns, it will be just like what happened in Sodom – when God rained down fire and brimstone and destroyed all the evil people. Read about it in Revelation 19:11-21.

Gāəthēs are too proud to accept the Bible's condemnation of homsx in the simplicity that God gave it. So they came up with their own reasons why God destroyed Sodom –

Was it because of weaponized anal rape?
Gāəthēs say that during the time of Sodom, men would dominate and humiliate other men by anally raping them. It was done to soldiers captured in war and to strangers who wandered into town. Gāəthēs say – that's the homsx God destroyed Sodom for – not modern homsx relates that are loving and intimate.

Gāəthēs are saying God would have applauded the men of Sodom if they'd showed up at Lot's door with flowers and chocolates to woo the angels – and invited the angels out to dinner and a drive-in movie – not for a one-night stand, but with the hope of a longterm relate.

Really? Is that what you'll tell God when He asks you why you showed up gay on Judgment Day?

The men of Sodom must have been super devoted to doing their duty of anally raping strangers. The angels blinded them, but they still kept trying to find Lot's door. They must have been thinking – these guys just blinded us, and we hate sticking our penises in men's anuses, but somebody's gotta teach these tourists a lesson. Genesis 19:11

The problem with that interp is the Bible never mentions weaponized anal rape. There's no cross references we could use as evidence that the men of Sodom had that as their motivation. That arg comes entirely from outside the Bible. Therefore, it's illegitimate to try and create a good homsx from it.

And of course, there are no romantic homsx relates in the Bible.

To get the right interp of Sodom, you have to look for it in the Bible.

Was it because of a lust for angels?
Jude 1:7 says the men of Sodom went after strange flesh. Gāəthēs say strange flesh means angel flesh. They claim the Sodomites weren't looking for sex with men – they wanted to have sex with angels.

No. The strange flesh they went after was sex with men. That's strange flesh because God said men must only have sex with women.

The Sodomites didn't even know Lot's guests were angels. The angels disguised their identity. When Genesis 18:22 tells us the angels went to Sodom, it says the men went to Sodom.

The Sodomites lusted after the male form. They said to Lot –

> Where are the men you took to your house tonight?
> Bring them out so we can have sex with them.
> Genesis 19:5

It wouldn't have mattered if Lot's guests were Fuddy M'Guddy and his buddy from the planet Crackmole. The Sodomites would have wanted them because they appeared to be beautiful young men – not because they were from Crackmole.

It wouldn't matter if they were Itching Papules from the planet Floptoast. They were fresh meat.

And the city was already doomed before Lot's angels arrived in Genesis 19. God told Abraham in Genesis 18:20-23 that He was going to destroy Sodom because their sin was very grievous. God sent the two angels to rescue Abraham's nephew, Lot. Genesis 19:15-16

Deuteronomy 29:23 says there were three other cities that God destroyed along with Sodom. They were Gomorrah, Admah, and Zeboim. There was another city called Zoar. But God spared it at Lot's request. That means there were five cities God wanted to destroy.
Genesis 19:17-23

If God condemned them because of angel sex, it would mean those five cities were resort towns for gay angels. There had to be hundreds of angels sneaking out of Heaven and flying to those cities to have sex with earth men.

The Bible says nothing about angels visiting those cities before God decided to destroy them. It means the evil thing they were doing that God killed them for was not sex with angels. It was men having sex with men, a lot. And it had been going on for a while. The incident at Lot's wasn't their first time.

Even if the men of Sodom wanted to have sex with Lot's visitors because they were angels, it would still be the abomination of homsx. Why? Because all the angels in the Bible are male.

Jude 1:6 mentions the bad angels in Genesis 6:4. They left Heaven to have sex with humans. Gāəthēs say it proves that the context of the condemnation of Sodom in the next verse, Jude 1:7, is sex with angels, not homsx.

No. Jude 1:5,6, and 7 are one. Verse 5 is about people God destroyed because of their unbelief. They had nothing to do with angels. In those three verses, Jude gave three examples of those who were punished by God for doing evil things.

So, the context in Jude 1:5,6, and 7 is not angels. The context is that God made examples of all three.

And the sons of God in Genesis 6:4 were hetsx angels. They had sex with women. There are no gay angels in the Bible.

Was it because they lacked hospitality?
When Jesus sent His disciples to various cities, He told them – if a city welcomes you, then bless that city. But, if a city won't welcome you, then you should wipe the dust of that city off yourselves. And on Judgment Day, that city will receive more condemnation than Sodom.
Luke 10:1-12

Gāəthēs say – see, Jesus compared Sodom to the cities that wouldn't welcome His disciples. So, that means God destroyed Sodom because they didn't welcome visitors, not because of homsx.

No. When Jesus sent the disciples, He told them –

> Whoever hears you, hears Me.
> And whoever rejects you, rejects Me.
> Jesus, Luke 10:16

That's because Jesus sent His disciples to say this –

> The kingdom of God
> has drawn near to you.
> Jesus, Luke 10:9

Jesus meant their Savior has drawn near to them – Jesus Christ, the only one who can get them into the kingdom of God. Jesus mentioned Sodom to make a point, by comparison. Everyone knows what the worst is – it's Sodom. But rejecting Jesus is even worse than Sodom.

Would the people in those cities have gone to Heaven if they rejected Jesus but invited His disciples in for lunch? No. If the Sodomites practiced hospitality, would God have let them do homsx? No.

Hospitality can't buy you Heaven or homsx.

The Bible tells us why God destroyed Sodom
Jude 1:7 says the men of Sodom engaged in sexual immorality, not inhospitality. The KJV says they – gave themselves over to fornication. That's just one word in the original Greek.

The word is ekporneuo.

Normally, when the Bible talks about sexual immorality, it uses the word porneia. But a much stronger word was needed to describe the extreme sexual immorality of the Sodomites. So, the word ek was attached to porneia to make porneia stronger.

Ekporneuo is a special word. It appears only once in the NT – here in Jude 1:7 to describe the horrifying behavior of the Sodomites.

God killed the Sodomites for ek-porneia, not xenophobia.

But the Gāəthēs have another arg. They say, well, you know, Jude did say the men of Sodom were guilty of ekporneuo, but there's lots of kinds of porneia. There's adultery, incest, and sex with animals. Jude didn't specify which one he meant. So we can't say it was homsx.

I can. Did the men pound on Lot's door and say – bring out your sheep so we can have sex with them? No. Did they say bring out your daughters? No. They said – bring out the two men. That's homsx.

God killed them all because they either did homsx or approved of it. They attended Sodom's gay pride parades. The Sodom Supreme Court legalized smsx marriage. They taught children that homsx is just as good as hetsx. And finally God had enough. Sudden destruction.

Was it because they didn't help the poor?
In Ezekiel 16:49-50, God said He killed the Sodomites because they –

- were proud
- became haughty and looked down on others
- had more food than they could eat
- but didn't help the poor and needy
- had a false feeling of peace and security
- committed abomination

Gāəthēs say – homsx is not on the list – so, God destroyed them because they didn't help the poor and needy, not because of homsx.

No, that's not true because Jude 1:7 told us God destroyed them because they gave themselves over to ekporneuo. Ezekiel's list is a step by step. They were proud of their wealth, then haughty, and then they committed abomination.

> The wealth of fools will destroy them.
> Proverbs 1:32

Gāəthēs say Ezekiel didn't tell us which abomination it was, so we can't say it's homsx. No, Ezekiel didn't need to tell us which abomination it was. Moses already told us in Genesis 19 – men pursuing sex with men. Ezekiel told us how the Sodomites got to Genesis 19.

> Pride leads to destruction,
> and a haughty spirit leads to a fall.
> Proverbs 16:18

Chapter twenty-three

Where's Jesus of the Gāəthēs?

People will say – look!
Christ is over there!
Christ is over here!
Don't believe them.
Those are fake Christs.
    Jesus, Matthew 24:23-24

We found him in the GRV –

> Jesus of the Gāəthēs said it's not what
> goes in your mouth that makes you unholy.
>
> When he said that, Jesus of the Gāəthēs
> declared all penises clean.
> > Matthew 15:11; Mark 7:19 GRV
> > Gāəthē Revised Version of the Bible
>
> The disciples of Jesus of the Gāəthēs said,
> teacher, explain that proverb to us. And he said –
>
> It doesn't matter what a person puts in their mouth.
> They can eat rats, bats, dogs, and snakes if they want to.
> And a man can put his friend's penis in his mouth.
>
> When a man puts his friend's penis in his mouth,
> his friend's penis isn't long enough to reach his heart.
>
> God doesn't care about what's in your mouth.
> He cares about what's in your heart.
> > Jesus of the Gāəthēs,
> > Matthew 15:15-18 GRV
> > Gāəthē Revised Version of the Bible

Our very own Bəthē got an interview –

Bəthē – So, you're Jesus of the Gāəthēs.

JotG – My followers call me Seth the lord.

Bəthē – I'm not saying that.

JotG – Then call me JotG.

Bəthē – Okay, JotG. Thank you for speaking with me.

JotG – No problem. How can I help you?

Bəthē – God's laws in the Old Testament clearly state that a man must never put rats, bats, or penises in his mouth.   Leviticus 11:1-23,41-47

JotG – I know.

Bəthē – Then why do you say it's okay?

JotG – Your Jesus did away with those laws.

Bəthē – No, He didn't.

JotG – He did away with them with a proverb.

Bəthē – What proverb?

JotG – Things that go in your mouth won't make you unholy.
Matthew 15:11

Bəthē – You're taking it out of context.

JotG – Can I ask you a question?

Bəthē – Sure.

JotG – Does God care if people have red hair?

Bəthē – No.

JotG – Why not?

Bəthē – Because hair doesn't matter.

JotG – What does matter?

Bəthē – The heart.

JotG – Bingo.

Bəthē – Bingo?

JotG – It's a game of chance. We play it at our church.

Bəthē – I'm sure you do. What's your point?

JotG – Your hair doesn't touch your heart.

Bəthē – Do you want to know the real meaning of that proverb?

JotG – I know the meaning. Jesus was concerned about the pain and suffering gay people experience because of Old Testament laws. So, He did away with them. Jesus combined pity and practicality. He rejected an antiquated set of laws so gay people could have love too.

Bəthē – JotG. What happened that led Jesus to say that proverb?

JotG – What?

Bəthē – An incident with the Pharisees.   Matthew 15:1-20; Mark 7:1-23

JotG – Jesus wasn't happy with them.

Bəthē – Why?

JotG – They were legalists.

Bəthē – How so?

JotG – They wanted gay people to obey Old Testament laws.

Bəthē – No. It wasn't that. The Pharisees made up a hand-washing ritual. They thought it washed off unholiness. But it was meaningless superstition. And they oppressed the people by making them do it too. That's why Jesus wasn't happy with the Pharisees.

JotG – So, it was about the hand-washing ritual, not gay people obeying Old Testament laws.

Bəthē – Bingo.

JotG – Good one.

Bəthē – Jesus defined the legalism of the Pharisees this way –

> You've gotten very good at forgetting
> where you put God's commandments
> so you can enforce your folklore instead.
> Jesus, Mark 7:9

Jesus quoted Isaiah 29:13 –

> They worship Me in vain
> because they teach the commandments of men
> as though they're My commandments.
> Jesus, Matthew 15:9

JotG – No, you're wrong, Bəthē. In Mark 7:15, Jesus said there's nothing that can enter a person that can make them unholy.

Bəthē – Remember the context, JotG. Jesus said that to let the people know they would not be putting unholiness in their mouths if they didn't perform the Pharisees' hand-washing ritual before they ate.

JotG – But it's about the heart.

Bəthē – Yes, it is. Jesus described the Pharisees this way –

> They draw near to Me with their words,
> but their hearts are far from Me.
> Jesus, Matthew 15:8, quoted from Isaiah 29:13

The Pharisees had a religion that was external. It was all for show – just a bunch of rituals and fancy costumes.

The Pharisees were a frequent foil for Jesus when He taught the people that true religion is not on the outside, but in the heart.

It's a lot easier to perform a bunch of meaningless rituals than it is to truly give your heart to God, and then obey Him. If you don't obey God, then you don't have a heart for God. All you have is phony sentimentality. God hates that.

You red hair analogy is false. God never said thou shalt not have red hair. But He did say men must not put pigs and penises in their mouth.

JotG – What's the harm in washing your hands before you eat?

Bəthē – The Pharisees thought they were washing off sin. But you can't get cleansed from sin your way – by making up a hand-washing ritual. You have to go to God and do it His way. When you do give your heart to God, then God works with you to cleanse you of sin. Jesus used this incident to teach us that the real cause of sin and unholiness is the evil desires of our hearts.

JotG – In many Bibles, Mark 7:19 says Jesus declared all foods clean.

Bəthē – Jesus never declared all foods clean. Why would God make pigs clean? For what purpose? That makes no sense.

Jesus didn't do away with the Old Testament laws. That wouldn't be pity or practicality. God's laws are a blessing. Obeying them promotes life and happiness.   Psalm 19:7-14; 119:1-176;
Matthew 5:17-28

It still wrong for a man to put a penis in his mouth and always will be. Disobeying God's laws brings misery and death. Deuteronomy 28:1-68

And it's still wrong to put a mouse in your mouth.

The correct translation of Mark 7:19 is in the King James Version.

JotG – Bəthē!

Bəthē – What?

JotG – Come up for air!

Bəthē – Excuse me?

JotG – Get your head out of the books. Too much learning has twisted your mind and made you crazy.

Bəthē – I'm not crazy. I speak words of truth, clearly and sanely.

JotG – Peace be with you.

Bəthē – Peace is always with me, and for me.   John 14:27

More JotG in the GRV –

> One day, Jesus of the Gāəthēs was hanging out
> in the cornfields with his disciples.
> And the Pharisees found two of his male disciples
> hiding in the corn and having sex.
>
> The Pharisees asked JotG why his disciples were
> doing something that was forbidden by
> the Old Testament law. And JotG said –
>
> If you knew that God wants people to be merciful
> then you would not have condemned the innocent.
> Matthew 12:1-2,7 GRV
> Gāəthē Revised Version of the Bible

Once again, here's JotG and Bəthē –

JotG – What's wrong, Bəthē?

Bəthē – Do you know what happened in Matthew 12?

JotG – Jesus let His disciples have gay sex.

Bəthē – Will you go through Matthew 12 with me?

JotG – Sounds like fun.

Bəthē – Read Matthew 12:1 in my Bible and tell me what it says.

JotG – It says the disciples were in a field eating someone's corn.

Bəthē – Then what happened?

JotG – The Pharisees saw them.

Bəthē – What did the Pharisees say to Jesus?

JotG – They said His disciples were doing something unlawful.

Bəthē – But it was lawful to eat the corn.

JotG – Right, as long as they didn't take any corn with them.
$$\text{Deuteronomy 23:25}$$

Bəthē – What was the Pharisees' problem?

JotG – It was the sabbath day.

Bəthē – And?

JotG – The fourth commandment forbids working on the sabbath day.
$$\text{Exodus 20:8-11}$$

Bəthē – What work did they accuse them of doing?

JotG – They had to pick the ears of corn from the stalks. Then they had to remove the outer coverings from the ears to get to the kernels.

Bəthē – Did Jesus tell His disciples to stop eating the corn?

JotG – No.

Bəthē – Why not?

JotG – Because Jesus was a lawbreaker.

Bəthē – No. Jesus obeyed God's law and the Roman government's law.

JotG – Oh.

Bəthē – Let's just go on. What happened next?

JotG – Jesus said to the Pharisees – haven't you read what David did?

Bəthē – What did David do?

JotG – He went into the tabernacle and ate bread.

Bəthē – It was holy bread that only the priests were supposed to eat.
                                        Leviticus 24:5-9; 1 Samuel 21:2-6

JotG – Why did David do that?

Bəthē – David had no other food to eat. He was on the run because king Saul was trying to kill him.   1 Samuel 19:9-12

JotG – Why did Jesus tell the Pharisees about David eating the bread?

Bəthē – It was the same thing as His disciples eating the corn.

JotG – How could His disciples be hungry like David? They weren't being hunted by a murderous king.

Bəthē – Mark 6:31 says the disciples had no time to eat.

JotG – Why not?

Bəthē – I'll tell you in a second. Read the next verse.

JotG – Right. Then Jesus told the Pharisees that the Old Testament law says priests have to go into the temple on the sabbath day of rest, and do the same work that they do on the other six days of the week.

Bəthē – But the priests would be innocent.

JotG – Absolutely. Oh, this is fun.

Bəthē – God's Word is delicious.   Jeremiah 15:16

JotG – So, what point is Jesus making?

Bəthē – Who said David could eat the bread he wasn't supposed to eat?

JotG – Who?

Bəthē – God did. When David came to Ahimelech to ask for the bread, Ahimelech asked God about David. That means God said okay.
1 Samuel 22:9-10,14-15

JotG – Why did God make an exception for David?

Bəthē – God chose David to be the king of Israel instead of Saul (the people's choice). God said David was a man after His own heart. David served the Lord faithfully. He was a believer. He worked for God.
1 Samuel 8:4-22; 9:15-17; 13:13-14; 16:1-13;
1 Kings 9:4-5; 15:1-3; Acts 13:21-22

JotG – What does all of this have to do with the disciples eating corn?

Bəthē – Who said the priests could work on the sabbath?

JotG – God?

Bəthē – Yes. God commanded them to. They worked for God.
Numbers 28:9-10

JotG – Where are you going with this, Bəthē?

Bəthē – After Jesus gave the Pharisees the two examples of David and the priests, Jesus said there's Someone greater than the temple.

JotG – Who?

Bəthē – Jesus is greater. The temple was God's house on earth. But now God Himself was on earth in a new Temple, a human body. Jesus was the reality that the temple symbolized. Only God Himself is greater than God's house. When Jesus said He is greater than the temple, He said He is God.
Matthew 12:6; Mark 14:55-59; 15:29-30;
John 2:18-22; Hebrews 9:8-12

JotG – Let me guess – the disciples had no time to eat because they were so busy working for Jesus, which means they worked for God.

Bəthē –They were the new priests working for God on the sabbath. That's why Jesus told the Pharisees that His disciples were innocent.

JotG – What work were the disciples doing?

Bəthē – They taught people how to receive salvation through Jesus.

JotG – Oh.

Bəthē – The disciples were not having sex.

JotG – I know.

Bəthē – Then why did you say they were?

JotG – I was making a point.

Bəthē – What point?

JotG – God believes in mercy.

Bəthē – Affirming someone's sin is not mercy. The disciples performed the greatest act of mercy when they did the work of teaching people to repent of sin and turn to the Savior, Jesus Christ.

So, JotG, do you want Jesus to save you?

JotG – No.

Bəthē – But you said studying the Bible study was fun.

JotG – It was, but –

Bəthē – But, what?

JotG – I love being worshiped by my followers.

Chapter twenty-four

Is Jesus inclusive?

They will say to the
mountains and rocks
– fall on us and hide us
from the face of Him
Who sits on the throne,
and from the fierce anger
of the Lamb, Jesus Christ.
                Revelation 6:16

You let gay people join your church, and you never tell them that homsx is sin. So, the world applauds you for being inclusive.

Suppose someone came to the door of your church covered in feces. Would you show them to a seat? No? Oh, so you're not inclusive. What if someone came to your church with their genitals exposed? Would you let them in? No? So you do have standards.

Ridiculous, you say? Not to God. The way you feel about the feces and genitals guys is the way God feels about unrepentant sexually immoral people being made members of a Christian church.

What if a member of your church comes to the Sunday service with his father's wife. And after the service you see the two of them sitting in a car, kissing passionately, mouth to mouth, with tongue. That man is a member of your church. Will you remain silent, or will you tell him it's a sin? Will you say – stop doing that or get out? Yes?

Then why are you inclusive to homsx? Why one and not the other? God said homsx is as bad as a man having sex with his father's wife.

> If a man has sex with his father's wife,
> both of them shall surely be put to death.
> God, Leviticus 20:11

> If a man has sex with another man
> as though that other man is a woman,
> both of those men have committed an abomination.
> They shall surely be put to death.
> God, Leviticus 20:13

Inclusion sounds nice. But it's mindless posturing.

Do you want practicing rapists or murderers to join your church and not change? No? Well, God said we all have to reform our lives. Homsxls too. Homsxls aren't special. You might say, well, we don't consider homsx to be a sin. Really? Do you consider it a sin for a man to have sex with his father's wife? Yes?

Then you're the one who's intolerant – of true teachings.

Paul said you'd come along –

> The day will come when the
> masqueraders in your midst will
> no longer tolerate true teachings.
> They'll satisfy their forbidden sexual
> desires by finding teachers who will
> whisper sweet affirmations in their ears.
> They'll turn away from the truth,
> and listen to lies instead.
> 2 Timothy 4:3-4

Is Jesus inclusive?
No! Never! Jesus congratulated the church in Ephesus for their noninclusiveness, their intolerance, their narrow-mindedness, their divisiveness. Were they racists? No! God welcomes those who love Him from every race and nation.   Acts 10:34-35

Jesus commended the church in Ephesus because they were intolerant of unrepentant sinners becoming members of their church –

> I know you won't tolerate evil people.
> Jesus, Revelation 2:2

The church in Corinth tolerated an incestuous member. Paul said –

> Put away from among yourselves
> that wicked person.
> 1 Corinthians 5:13 KJV

Would a gay-rights group hire someone who says homsx is sin? No? Then why do you vilify a church for not granting membership to a practicing homsxl? Why can others have standards but not Christians?

> Welcome to
>
> The First Church in Corinth.
>
> We are an inclusive
>
> incest-affirming congregation.
>
> All love is love.

Jesus rebuked the church in Thyatira for being inclusive –

> I have this against you.
> You let Jezebel join your church.
> And now she's seducing My servants
> by telling them she speaks for God.
> She's teaching them to practice porneia
> and to eat food that was sacrificed to idols.
> And you sit back and do nothing about it.
>
> I gave her some time so she'd have a chance
> to repent of her porneia. But she wouldn't.
>
> Listen carefully.
> If Jezebel and her lovers don't stop it,
> then I'll make all of them lie down together
> in a bed of unbearable misery.
>
> And I will destroy those who inherit her business.
> They will die – death upon death
>
> Jesus, Revelation 2:20-23

The world loves you because you're inclusive. But that love came at a big price. It cost you Jesus.

> The Corinthian Church
>
> invites you to join us
>
> as we march in this year's
>
> Incest Pride Parade.
>
> Show your love and support
>
> for the incest community.
>
> Free incest pride flags
>
> for the kids!
>
> "Love one another"
>
> – Jesus, John 15:12

Chapter twenty-five

What's a J•Lite?

Listen to Me.
A day is coming that will burn like an oven.
When all the proud, and yes,
all who do wickedly, will be stubble.
The day that's coming will burn them up,
says the Lord of Heaven's army.
It will leave them neither root nor branch.

But to you who reverence Me,
the Sun of righteousness will arise
with healing in His wings.
You will go forth,
and grow up like calves of the stall.

And you will tread down the wicked.
They will be ashes under the soles of your feet,
in the day that I will do this,
says the Lord of Heaven's army.
    God, Malachi 4:1-3

J•Lite – Hi. I'm a J•Lite.

Bəthē – What's a J•Lite?

J•Lite – A follower of Jesus Lite.

Bəthē – What do you do?

J•Lite – We give out free hugs and lip balm.

Bəthē – Who's Jesus Lite?

J•Lite – He's a new Jesus for people who don't like the old Jesus.

Bəthē – Why don't you like the Jesus of the Bible?

J•Lite – He's too Old Testament – so in-your-face and demanding. That just turns people off. And He's rude, and kind of judgmental. Where's the love in that?

Bəthē – Can you give me an example?

J•Lite – Listen to this –

> People who just pretend to follow Me will be thrown aside like branches that broke off a tree. And after they've dried up, they'll be gathered together and thrown into the fire to be burned.
> Jesus, John 15:6

Who would follow someone who said that?

Bəthē – Jesus also said –

> If anyone rejects Me and My words, then I will reject them when I return with the holy angels in My glory and in My Father's glory.
> Jesus, Luke 9:26

Those words of Jesus that you've rejected are a warning about hell. Doesn't Jesus Lite warn you about hell?

J•Lite – Jesus Lite preaches love.

Bəthē – Doesn't he teach you about sin?

J•Lite – Jesus Lite said the only sin is to think you know the truth.

And Jesus Lite promises to not hurt your feelings by committing the greatest sin of all – claiming you know it's an absolute truth from the Bible that homosexuality is a sin. It's deeply offensive to Jesus Lite when people do that. It makes him sad. Jesus Lite has evolved.

Bəthē – The Bible says homosexuality is a sin.

J•Lite – You Bəthēs are like boys in a tree house with a sign that says No Girls Allowed. You only want straight people in Heaven, so you put up a No Gays Allowed sign. Jesus doesn't just welcome straight people into Heaven. He welcomes gay people too.

Bəthē – First Corinthians 6:9 says homosexuals won't go to Heaven.

J•Lite – The word homosexuals in that verse is an English translation of the Greek words malakoi and arsenokoites. The word arsenokoites didn't even exist in Greek literature. Paul just made it up. Nobody knows what it means.

Bəthē – Christians don't use Greek literature to interpret the Bible. In Leviticus 18:22 and 20:13, God used two Hebrew words to describe homosexuality – zakar, which means a man – and sakab, which means to lie down. Homosexuality is when a man lies down with a man.

The Greek word Paul used – arsenokoites, is made up of two smaller Greek words – arsen, which means a man – and koites, which means to lie down. Paul didn't make up the word arsenokoites. He got it from the Old Testament. It's the Greek version of the Hebrew words in Leviticus. It means a man who lies down with another man to have sex.

J•Lite – If you only use the Bible, then you have a problem.

Bəthē – Why do you say that?

J•Lite – The word malakoi appears only one other time in the Bible. It's when Jesus said John the Baptist did not wear soft clothing. Malakoi doesn't mean homosexuality – it means soft.   Matthew 11:8; Luke 7:25

Bəthē – We know arsenokoites means homosexuality. So, when Paul put malakoi together with arsenokoites in 1 Corinthians 6:9, and said they won't go to Heaven, we know Paul was using the word malakoi for the soft man, the one who plays the role of the woman in an act of homosexual intercourse. The malakoi is the man who lets his anus be used like a vagina by another man.

J•Lite – Then why did Paul use the word malakoi, which means soft? Why didn't he say – a man who lets his anus be used like a vagina by another man won't go to Heaven?

Bəthē – The Bible puts it in more polite language.

No one goes to hell for wearing silk pajamas. But men do go to hell if they don't stop letting another man stick his penis in their anus. Is it worth dying for? Is it worth missing out on eternity in Heaven?

J•Lite – Jesus loves gay people just the way they are.

Bəthē – You're not telling the whole truth. Yes, Jesus feels so much love for gay people – just the way they are – that He died on a cross to save them. But Jesus doesn't love sin. You want Heaven without repentance. Before gay people can be saved there has to be a change of heart. They have to acknowledge that homosexuality is sin, and turn to Jesus with a desire to obey Him.   1 John 2:2

J•Lite – So, Jesus won't love gay people just the way they are?

Bəthē – Jesus will love them – all the way to hell.

J•Lite – You need to stop telling gay people that they're sinning. Jesus said the greatest commandment is to love your neighbor.

Bəthē – No, that's the second greatest commandment.

J•Lite – What's the first?

Bəthē – Jesus said the first greatest commandment is to love the Lord your God with all your heart, all your soul, all your mind, and all your strength. If you don't obey the first greatest commandment, then you can't obey the second greatest commandment.   Mark 12:30-31

J•Lite – Why not?

Bəthē – Because you're not using your mind. When Jesus said love your neighbor, He was quoting Leviticus 19:18. The previous verse, Leviticus 19:17, says you're not supposed to hate your neighbor in your heart. It says you hate your neighbor when you approve of a bad thing they're doing and don't tell them that what they're doing is wrong.

Love warns. If your neighbor is about to drink poison and you don't warn them, then you're a murderer.   Ezekiel 3:18-19

J•Lite   If you care so much about Leviticus, why do you disobey it? You use Leviticus 20:13 to condemn homosexuality. But it calls for the death penalty. If you're such a biblical literalist, then why aren't you executing homosexuals?

Bəthē – Will you accuse the apostle Paul?

J•Lite – What did he do?

Bəthē – Leviticus 20:11 says a man who has sex with his father's wife is to be executed.

But when a man in the Corinthian church was sleeping with his father's wife, Paul didn't say take him out and stone him. He said kick the man out of your church.   1 Corinthians 5:1-13

You're mocking God's mercy. Jesus died on a cross so we can be forgiven for our sins if we turn to Him. Paul said a fellow Christian is to be forgiven and welcomed back when they change their mind.
2 Corinthians 2:4-11

Homosexuality is still a death penalty offense. The difference now is that God carries out the executions – in hell.   Revelation 20:15

J•Lite – You're sick. All this talk about hell.

Bəthē – Jesus said it's better to cut off your right hand and pluck out your right eye than to go to hell with two hands and two eyes. He meant you should cut off and pluck out of your life even the most precious person or thing if they're leading you to hell.
Matthew 5:29-30

J•Lite – You're making God out to be a prude. God approved of men having more than one wife. King Solomon had a thousand wives. So how could God have a problem with a man having one husband?
1 Kings 11:3

Bəthē – God said the king must not have many wives. God didn't create polygamy and He didn't approve of it. It's a perversion of God's standard. The first one who did polygamy was a man named Lamech.
Genesis 4:19-23-24; Deuteronomy 17:17

J•Lite – God never punished David or Solomon for their polygamy.

Bəthē – You're mocking God again. You're accusing Him of being unjust because you think He didn't punish David, or Solomon, or any of the other men who disobeyed Him by having more than one wife. All sin has consequences.

Be sure your sin will find you out.
God, Numbers 32:23 KJV

J•Lite – Oh really? It's right there in Numbers 32:23, is it? And nobody ever gets anything wrong that they read in the Bible, do they?

Bəthē – What are you talking about?

J•Lite – It says in the Bible that God made the sun stand still for twenty-four hours so Joshua's army could defeat their enemy.
Joshua 10:12-14

For hundreds of years Christians read that and thought it meant the sun revolves around the earth. They said – it's right there in the Bible. But when the telescope was invented, people saw that they got it wrong, that the earth revolves around the sun.

You say it's right there in the Bible – homosexuality is a sin. But if you had a telescope, then you'd see that you got it wrong too.

Bəthē – There's a simple answer. The reason God said He made the sun stand still is because that's how it appears to us.

God won't send you to hell if you think He said the sun revolves around the earth. But He will send you to hell if you think He said homosexuality is not a sin. You don't need a telescope to know that. You need an obedient heart.

> I enjoy looking down from Heaven to watch a humble person – the one who admits they have no hope without Me, and who cares anxiously about what I said in the Bible.
> God, Isaiah 66:2

J•Lite – Maybe Leviticus does say homosexuality is a sin. But Leviticus also says don't eat shrimp, don't plant two different kinds of seeds in the same field, and don't wear a shirt made of two different fabrics.

Bəthē – Is this your argument? –

- God said homosexuality is a sin
- God also said don't eat shrimp
- Therefore, God meant homosexuality is not a sin

J•Lite – Something like that.

Bəthē – You trick people into thinking homosexuality is harmless by comparing it to things in Leviticus that sound harmless to them. You don't show them the laws in Leviticus that condemn adultery, incest, child sacrifice, and cursing your father and mother.
Leviticus 11:9-12; 19:19; 20:5-13

J•Lite – Most Christians eat shrimp.

Bəthē – You want God to let you be gay because people eat shrimp?

J•Lite – Exactly.

Bəthē – Suppose Eve said – yes, God, I ate from the tree. But yesterday I saw Adam planting two different seeds in the same field. God would not have said – oh, in that case, nevermind. He would have said – I told you, if you eat, you die. You ate, and you will die.
Genesis 5:5

And by the way, myself, and many of my fellow Christians obey the law that says don't eat shrimp.
Leviticus 11:9-12

J•Lite – Jesus would bless same-sex marriages. He reinvented family.

Bəthē – What makes you say that?

J•Lite – One time when Jesus was meeting with His disciples, He was told that His mother, brothers, and sisters wanted to see Him. But Jesus said His disciples were His mother, brothers, and sisters.

Bəthē – Jesus said those who are hearing the Word of God and doing what it says are His mother, brothers, and sisters.
Luke 8:21

He was making the point that obeying God is the most important thing – even more important than our love for our family. You're not obeying God if you approve of same-sex marriages.

J•Lite – In Matthew 19:11, Jesus said people can't be celibate if they're not called to it. You're disobeying Jesus when you say all gay people have to be celibate. All gay people aren't called to it.

Gay Christians experience pain, sadness, and loneliness because people like you forbid them from marrying. They just want the same thing that straight Christians want – love and intimacy.

Bəthē – Straights can't make up any kind of marriage we want either. Christians don't cry because we can't sin sexually. Jesus said if you want to follow Him, then you have to deny yourself and take up your cross daily. The cross means death. Christians die to self.

Luke 9:23; 14:25-27

Jesus told Peter that he would be executed for following Him. Peter didn't say – that really isn't fair, Lord. My wife and me were looking forward to spending our sunset years together. We even bought a little place on the coast so I can do some fishing.   John 21:18-19

Peter said – yes Lord – by living his life for Jesus.

And he didn't write a book to complain about how Jesus wouldn't let him grow old with his wife. He wasn't invited to churches to explain why Jesus should have let him live to a hundred. In one of his epistles, Peter matter-of-factly referred to his execution as his exodus. He faced his execution the same way Jesus faced His – he set his face like flint.

2 Peter 1:15

Jesus was a young man when He gave His life for us. He didn't whine that He missed out on getting married.

It's an honor for Christians to give up our own desires for our Lord and Savior, Jesus Christ. He said – no gay sex, and we say – yes, Lord. And if God wants us to lose our lives for Jesus, we say – yes, Lord.

Jesus never complained about giving up His life for us.   Isaiah 50:6-7

J•Lite – So, involuntary celibacy for gay people?

Bəthē – Celibacy for all unlawful sex.

Thank God for telling you not to be gay. Being gay is deadly, physically and spiritually.

Deuteronomy 28:58-61

J•Lite – Will you come to our church?

Bəthē – What does your church do?

J•Lite – We give out food in Harvard Square.

Bəthē – Do you give them the Gospel?

J•Lite – No.

Bəthē – Why not?

J•Lite – Too bloody.

Bəthē – Our sins could only be paid for by the shedding of blood. Jesus made the full payment for our sins when He died on a cross.

Hebrews 9:22-28

J•Lite – That sounds awful.

Bəthē – It's the Gospel, the Good News.

J•Lite – We don't see a need for the Good News.

Bəthē – That's because you haven't heard the bad news.

J•Lite – What's the bad news?

Bəthē – God's punishment for sin.   Revelation 20:15; 21:7-8

J•Lite – We make the Gospel more humane.

Bəthē – You do what?

J•Lite – Our church holds workshops to teach people how to deconstruct the Gospel so it won't offend gay people.

Bəthē – Why do you do that?

J•Lite – We want the church to be a welcoming place for people of all genders and sexual orientations.

Bəthē – You need to hear this –

> God condemns to death
> those who say evil is good and good is evil
> – who call bitter sweet and sweet bitter.
> God condemns to death
> those who think they know better than Him.
> Isaiah 5:20-21

J•Lite – The Bible only condemns bad homosexuality.

Bəthē – What makes it bad?

J•Lite – It's selfish and exploitive. Men forcing men to have sex.

Bəthē – Romans 1:27 doesn't say anything about forced sex. It says men do homosexuality because they burn in their lust for each other.

J•Lite – I don't go by an obscure passage in Romans. I go by the words of Jesus in the Sermon on the Mount. I go by Jesus, not Paul.

Bəthē – Paul was appointed by Jesus. Christians go by everything in the Sermon on the Mount and everything in the book of Romans.

Acts 9:15

Jesus said don't just be concerned with eating food so your temporary physical body can live. He said be concerned with eating every word that comes from the mouth of God so you can live in a perfect spiritual body for all eternity. That's every word, from Genesis to Revelation.

Matthew 4:4

J•Lite – There's a good kind of homosexuality.

Bəthē – Where's that in the Bible?

J•Lite – It's not in the Bible. It was just discovered by psychologists.

Bəthē – What makes it good?

J•Lite – It's loving and committed.

Bəthē – You can't make sin good by adding love and commitment.

J•Lite – When Moses wrote Leviticus he only had one model to go by. That's what he was condemning. You're asking the impossible. You want Leviticus to be about our modern, sophisticated homosexual relationships – something Moses knew nothing about.

Bəthē – Here's your argument – the Bible didn't say we can't do good homosexuality. Imagine the possibilities. The Bible condemns your sin? Then say – no, I'm doing the good version. That's precisely how the devil deceived Eve – he told her God never said she can't eat from the tree in the good way. Whatever new kind of homosexuality you come up with, the Bible condemns it.

J•Lite – I'm saying the Holy Spirit directed Moses to write those laws about homosexuality according to the facts at the time.

Bəthē – Why didn't the Holy Spirit tell Moses about the good homosexuality? Are you saying the Holy Spirit didn't know about it either? Did you tell the Holy Spirit about this good homosexuality? Maybe God can write an addendum to the Bible to tell people about it.

Your argument has no facts. The only evidence you can produce for your good homosexuality is that God forgot to put it in the Bible.

Good Homosexuality and Bad Homosexuality walk into a drugstore. They decide to sit at the soda fountain. But the soda jerk only brings one soda. So Bad Homosexuality says – excuse me, you forgot my buddy's soda. And the soda jerk says – hey pal, you came in here alone.

J•Lite – Moses didn't know any gay people. If he could have sat down and talked with some normal, responsible gay people, he would have seen that they're no different than anyone else, and he would have blessed their relationships.

Bəthē – What if a gay man is at the top of his class in school – what if he serves honorably in the military, is a war hero, saves the lives of his fellow soldiers? What if he goes into civil service, does good for the community, works at soup kitchens?

Will God say – I don't care if he's gay, he's too good to keep out of Heaven? No. Why not? Because of the sin problem. Trying to use good deeds to erase your sin is like trying to hand God a bloody tampon.
Isaiah 64:6

Moses would not have changed God's law because he talked to gay people. God doesn't care how nicely you sin. He doesn't excuse sin because you're a model citizen.

Then how does a good gay man get to Heaven? There's only one way. Repent of your homosexuality and receive Jesus Christ as your Lord and Savior.

J•Lite – Homosexuality is natural.

Bəthē – No, it isn't.

J•Lite – Then why do animals do it?

Bəthē – When Adam sinned, God told him –

> You listened to your wife,
> and she got you to eat from the tree I told you
> not to eat from. Now the land that produces
> your food is cursed because of you.
> God, Genesis 3:17

It wasn't just the soil that was cursed because of Adam's sin. Every person and all of nature are subjected to misery –

> All of nature moans together in pain, even now.
> Romans 8:22

There weren't any animals doing homosexuality in the Garden of Eden. Homosexuality is not natural or good because animals do it. They do it for the same reason humans do it – because of the sin that was brought into the world by Adam.   Romans 8:19-23

J•Lite – Homosexuality is okay now.

Bəthē – Says who?

J Lite – Jesus said the Holy Spirit will bring new truth. The Holy Spirit is trying to tell you something. He's whispering in your ear – trust Me, homosexuality is a holy sacrament.

God didn't go on vacation after He wrote the Bible. So stop clinging to your Bible and listen to the still, small voice. Never put an exclamation mark where God put an ellipsis. God is still talking.

Bəthē – A lot of people think of the Father, Jesus, and the Holy Spirit as though the Father is their earthly father, who is strict and a little scary, and Jesus is their mother, who is more lenient, and the Holy Spirit is their grandmother, who lets them do whatever they want.

So people say the Holy Spirit lets them yell out any nonsense that pops into their heads, or roll around on the floor laughing.

And some say the Holy Spirit lets them be gay.

In John 16:12, Jesus told the apostles that He had many more things to say to them but they weren't able to understand them now. He meant many more things about what He already taught them.   Mark 13:23

Then, in the next verse, John 16:13, Jesus told them the Holy Spirit will lead them to a more complete understanding of what He taught them.

Jesus had to stop teaching because He had to die. He came to earth so He could die in a human body as the sacrifice for sin. But He had more teaching to do. So, after Jesus rose from the dead and went back to Heaven, He came back to earth to teach believers in a new way – by living in our hearts.

> I will not leave you comfortless:
> I will come to you.
> Jesus, John 14:18 KJV

J•Lite – John 16:13 says the Holy Spirit will speak of things to come. It means the Holy Spirit tells us about the good homosexuality.

Bəthē – In John 16:13, Jesus said God's Holy Spirit will guide believers into all truth. Jesus said His Holy Spirit speaks what He hears. And in John 14:26, Jesus told us what God's Holy Spirit hears – it's the things that Jesus taught, the Word of God.

So, His Holy Spirit only teaches the Word of God. Therefore, God's Holy Spirit will not teach a good homosexuality because The Word of God never taught a good homosexuality. It's not part of all truth.

The things to come are the teachings in the New Testament written by the apostles and others under the direction of the Holy Spirit of Jesus. Those teachings are the same as the teachings of Jesus. There isn't any new truth that contradicts the old truth.   2 Peter 1:20-21

J•Lite – When you keep gay people out of your church, you're no different than white racists who want black people kept out of church.

Bəthē – In the beginning, when God created people, He looked at black people and said – very good. Genesis 1:26-27,31

But God didn't create gay people. When He saw what they were doing He said it was very bad, an abomination. So, comparing homosexuality to being black is a slander against God and an insult to black people.

J•Lite – God said pork is an abomination too. Christians love to use the word abomination for homosexuality, but not when they eat pork.

Bəthē – I don't eat pork. Leviticus 11:7

J•Lite – When the Bible says homosexuality is an abomination, it doesn't mean homosexuality is evil in itself. The Bible uses the word abomination to refer to things people didn't do because it was a custom of theirs not to do them.

For instance, Genesis 43:32 says the Egyptians considered it an abomination to eat a meal with Hebrews. It was just their custom.

Bəthē – Proverbs 6:16-19 lists seven things that God hates and that are an abomination to Him. Among the seven are lying and the shedding of innocent blood – things that are are evil in themselves.

J•Lite – Homosexuality is okay now because the law was done away.

Bəthē – Really? The law also says this –

> Don't cheat poor people out of justice in their legal cases.
>
> Don't execute a person for a crime they didn't commit.
>
> Don't torture foreigners who live in your country.
> God, Exodus 23:6,7,9

Are those things okay now?

J•Lite – Jesus did away with the law.

Bəthē – Jesus raised the level of respect for the law. He said you commit adultery when you go to bed with someone in your mind.

                                          Exodus 20:14; Matthew 5:27-28

J•Lite – You cause gay bashing when you say it's a sin to be gay.

Bəthē – Gay bashing happens for the same reason that anyone who's different gets picked on. It's because of the sinful nature we inherited from Adam. The only way people can control those evil urges is if they're transformed by hearing the Bible – every word.

J•Lite – Jesus lived with twelve men. And He had an unusually close relationship with His apostle, John. Have you ever considered the possibility that Jesus Himself might have been –

Bəthē – Stop right there. You're about to say something evil and I don't want to hear it. Jesus obeyed the Old Testament laws perfectly and absolutely. Jesus never sinned. He was the holiness of God walking around in a human body. Jesus is perfect.

J•Lite – I don't see anything wrong with being gay

Bəthē – It's easy to say that when you're young and healthy. There's a way to find out that gay people know it's a sin to be gay.

J•Lite – How?

Bəthē – Talk to them on their death bed.

J•Lite – You never answered my question.

Bəthē – Which one?

J•Lite – Will you come to church?

Bəthē – Tell me more about your church.

J•Lite – Jesus Lite wants new ideas.

Bəthē – Where does he get them?

J•Lite – He smells every wind.   Ephesians 4:14

Bəthē – What goes on at your church?

J•Lite – We dim the lights and play synthetic Christian music.

Bəthē – Then what?

J•Lite – Confetti falls from the ceiling.

Bəthē – And?

J•Lite – Clowns bounce beach balls into the crowd.

Bəthē – What else?

J•Lite – We're entertained by word jugglers.

Bəthē – Does anyone speak?

J•Lite – People come up and talk about their lives.

Bəthē – Does your pastor give a sermon?

J•Lite – Our pastor doesn't talk about his faith.

Bəthē – Can't the elders give the sermon?

J•Lite – The elders took a vow of silence.

Bəthē – Who gives the sermon?

J•Lite – The sermon is delivered by a mime.

Bəthē – Does the mime teach from the Bible?

J•Lite – We can't tolerate Bible teaching.

Bəthē – What does the mime teach?

J•Lite – Fables.

Bəthē – That's it? That's all you do for people?

J•Lite – No, there's one last thing.

Bəthē – What?

J•Lite – We give the pill to first-time visitors.

Bəthē – The pill?

J•Lite – The Christian pill.

Bəthē – What's in this Christian pill?

J•Lite – Salvation. We put salvation in a pill.

Bəthē – What does the pill do?

J•Lite – It makes you a Christian.

Bəthē – Is that right?

J•Lite – Yup. Just take the pill and you're a Christian.

Bəthē – So, that's what it's come to.

I've got some news for your church. I'll say it like I'm standing on a street corner hawking newspapers. Extra! Extra! Read all about it –

Jesus destroys the work of the devil!
1 John 3:8

www.ingramcontent.com/pod-product-compliance
Lightning Source LLC
Chambersburg PA
CBHW031443040426
42444CB00007B/951